It's All in Your Head

Managing Stress in Your Life

Duane Pajak

To Richard,
Thank you for the great review!
Remember, life is short so choose
the stress-free road on your journey.
Duane Pajak

Halo Publishing International

ISBN: 978-1-61244-221-1
Library of Congress Control Number: 2013918322

Printed in the United States of America

Halo Publishing International

Published by Halo Publishing International
AP# 726
P.O Box 60326
Houston, Texas 77205
Toll Free 1-877-705-9647
Website: www.halopublishing.com
E-mail: contact@halopublishing.com

This book is dedicated to my beautiful, loving wife, Maureen, whose love, inspiration, and endurance have motivated me to pursue my endeavor to help others in search of peace and happiness, and to our three sons, Kevin, Craig, and John who have always encouraged me to "go for it," when pursuing my goals in life.

Contents

Acknowledgments

My writing of this book on stress was inspired by the writings and advice of others. I would like to pay tribute to the late and great psychologist, Albert Ellis, for his ideas on living rationally in an irrational world, as discussed in his popular book, "A New Guide to Rational Living." I was especially inspired by the thoughts and ideas expressed in the highly influential books of the founders of, "The Three Principles," (formally known as, "Psychology of Mind"): Roger Mills, George Pransky, cousin of Jack Pransky, whose book, "Somebody Should Have Told Us," was inspirational, and to the late Sydney Banks and his philosophical ideas behind, "The Three Principles."

My ideas behind managing stress were particularly influenced by the writings of Joseph Bailey and Richard Carlson, especially their book, "Slowing Down to the Speed of Life," and Carlson's books like, "Don't Sweat the Small Stuff." As such, I am very grateful for the kind words and enthusiastic remarks of the late Richard Carlson's wife, Kris Carlson, and to Joseph Bailey for his other great books, "The Serenity Principle," and, "The Speed Trap." I would also like to credit the works of Andrew Weil, M.D., as exemplified in his book, "Spontaneous Happiness," and in his very peace of mind promoting CD, "Sound Body, Sound Mind...." and to other influential authors on the subject of stress and finding happiness, including: David Myers in his popular book, "The Pursuit of Happiness," and to Martin Seligman, the former president of the, American Psychological Association, for his practical and meaningful book, "Authentic Happiness," and to Thomas Kelley, and his remarkable, highly insightful and practical book, "Falling In Love With Life."

It took me a long time, but I finally found a publisher with a great heart and soul, one whose chemistry made for a great publisher-author relationship. Here I refer to and want to thank, Lisa Umina, wonderful publisher of Halo Publishing International, and to her great publishing team, especially the editor, Virginia Grenier. This publisher believed in my book and made it all possible; for that, I am truly grateful.

I am also thankful for my friends and colleagues who had some very significant and meaningful remarks to make about my book. My good friend, Jerry Blevins not only wrote a great testimonial of my book, but was also very helpful in his informal editing and commenting of my book's nature. Another individual I want to thank is Dale Herder for his wonderful testimonial. Dale is a college English professor, he is also an author. I appreciate his review of the manuscript and his support for its content. I especially appreciate his help with review of the book's structure and content.

I want to especially thank college president, Cameron Brunet-Koch for her very poignant, positive, and in-depth review, and the high-lighting of the book's true perspective and meaning, to encourage people to find "balance" in everyday life. Cameron was also instrumental in making several key suggestions for the book's content.

I want to thank retired psychiatrist, Phil Woollcott, for his positive comments on the book. There is also a great endorsement that I really appreciate from my colleague, Bill Nicholson, who has his own neuropsychological treatment center, and is President of the Michigan Psychological Association.

Finally, I want to thank Mary Lou Tanton, a retired elementary school teacher, for her great interpretation of the book's main message, and to attorney, Richard Clark, for his "outstanding" review and remarks about the book's stress reduction mission.

Preface

It goes without saying, "stress kills." Every day we hear about people dying from heart related conditions, strokes and unfortunately, drug and/or alcohol related episodes. We might say it is unfair to include drug and alcohol related problems with the more "physical" problems of cardiovascular diseases; many health experts believe both physical and mental conditions are "diseases." They both have causes, symptoms and classified diagnoses, and are subject to medical treatment.

However, while it is difficult to prove the exact reason behind any medical or psychological condition, many health experts believe one major cause is STRESS. Apparently, everyone experiences stress in his or her everyday life. It appears stress affects everyone from every age and walk of life. In addition, it seems stress is a natural part of human existence.

While we as individuals are subject to stress in our lives, there are those individuals who seem to cope or deal with stress more effectively than others. You might ask; "Why is that? Why are some people much more capable of facing down stress in its tracks, picking themselves up when problems or even tragedy strikes, and managing to find satisfaction and pleasure in life?" Others, on the other hand, resort to depression, chemical substances or even suicidal tendencies when stress brings them down.

Stress need not bring us down or put us in hopeless situations. There are ways to deal head on with the stress in our lives. We can all learn from others, from ancient philosophers, to early or modern day psychologists and psychiatrists, to scholars, to family physicians, to members of the clergy, to individual friends and family members. It's not that any one group or individual has all the answers, but any one person at any given time can do or say something that may affect how we think, feel or act.

It is possible to not only learn from others, but also look inward to ourselves to find answers or solutions to everyday problems. Yes, you yourself can find ways to deal with problems and the many stressors in your life. In essence, don't sell yourself short when faced with minor or major issues in your life. While it is good to learn from others and have a support group or network to rely on when facing life's battles, many of the problems in life can be dealt by finding your own inner strength and peace of mind.

A book like this can help! Books are not necessarily the solution to problems, but as guides or "tools" applied to life's problems. Many times, we can be annoyed or irritated with what may seem to be petty occurrences or issues, but they can build up inside ourselves to the point where we might just want to scream or lash out. Ideas in this book can help. We can use the ideas or suggestions laid forth in this and other books to face up to not only the minor annoyances in life, but to the more serious hurdles and conflicts in life as well.

Although you might find ideas or suggestions from books or individuals in your life to be helpful, they are not necessarily the panacea or the final solution to your problems. Furthermore, they may not reduce the impact of the stress in your life in a significant way. These ideas can be a starting point. They can help correct old habits or ways of thinking that may have contributed to your low moods. You will need to open your mind to the basic thoughts and ideas found in this book. You might be surprised on how useful the steps pointed out can be in addressing the minor and major stressors of your life. Give the book a chance to find reasons for the stress in your life and find better ways of coping or dealing with the stress.

As you browse through the chapter headings, you will see stress defined and addressed in simple, direct ways, but also put into a more positive light. I will give you ways to look at stress in a more positive way. You will be given constructive steps to address stress related problems and practical ways to find love and beauty in life.

This book is written with the ordinary person in mind. In other words, anyone from any profession or career can use the ideas in the book for self-help purposes, it is not a psychological textbook. Since the book is a self-help tool, it does not take the place of psychotherapy or other forms of treatment for mental health or substance related problems.

Many of the ideas in the book stem from two psychological theories: "Rational-Emotive Behavior Therapy (REBT)" as founded by Albert Ellis, and "Psychology of Mind" or now referred to as "The Three Principles" as founded by Sydney Banks, Roger Mills and George Pransky. Additionally, many of the ideas and suggestions from the book come from this author himself and from his vast experience as a clinical therapist and college professor.

You can use this book and the beautiful photos included to help find inner peace and outer beauty of a life you deserve. There are constructive ways to find sensation, excitement and exhilaration in life without depending on drugs, alcohol or other outside entertainment. Similarly, there are ways to find inner peace, a sense of calm and tranquility, without relying on chemical substances. The means to a happier, more fulfilling lifestyle are inside you. You can learn to live life in a more "inner" directed manner compared to a more "outer" driven one. In other words, you can choose to live life more fully by being more inner directed and less dependent on outside sources for satisfaction. Whether you realize it or not, you can find ways to reduce stress in your life by looking inward, to your God given strengths and skills.

Each of us is born with unique talents and the means to find happiness in life. All we need to do is not only, "wake up and smell the roses," but also live life in a more harmonious, self-fulfilling fashion. It is up to you to open your mind and learn to cope with stress in more positive, constructive ways, instead of dead-end, destructive ways.

Take a step forward with this book. Take a deep breath, let the negative energy go and simply enjoy the journey to a less stressful and more rewarding lifestyle.

Chapter 1

Stress Defined

There are several points of view to look at stress, including civil engineering. For example, the strength of the center span in a suspension bridge design. You can also define it from a psychological point of view, which is where this book comes in. A great Canadian scientist, Hans Selye suggested in 1936 that stress is a physiological response to external stresses. As such, stress can cause ulcers, heart-related problems and a host of other medical conditions. Selye is credited with a concept called, "General Adaption Syndrome" whereby an individual can go through three stages in reaction to stress: alarm, resistance and exhaustion. In addition to Selye's work, brain scientists have pinpointed the effects of stress on areas of the brain, our hormones and our neurotransmitters.

Given the remarkable work in the biomedical, psychological and psychiatric fields, we discovered much about how and why humans and animals alike seem to respond negatively to environmental stressors. The purpose of this book is not to describe the inner workings of the mind or to use a lot of technical jargon related to scientific research. For instance, there will be no detailed description of how the "Hypothalamic-Pituitary-Adrenocortical" (HPA) axis is activated during a person's stress experiences. While we can all recognize and appreciate how scientists have contributed to our understanding of psychological stress, we don't need charts, diagrams and technical language to help us figure out what stress is and how to deal with it.

Let's use the example of how someone defined pornography. He said something to the effect of, "I don't know what pornography is, but I know it when I see it." You can say the same for psychological stress: "I don't know what stress is, but I know it when I'm feeling it." While each of us might have our own definition of what stress is and of how it affects us, we can make it as simple or as complicated as we wish. According to James Coleman from his book, "Contemporary Psychology and Effective Behavior" (1979), and from my point of view, stress can simply be defined as, "adjustive demands placed upon us." In other words, when faced with the challenges of what we may think stress is, we feel pressure in some way to "adjust" to the stressful situation.

In order for us to come to grips with adjusting to the demands facing us, we might find it helpful to clarify the kinds and types of stressors we may be experiencing at any given moment. According to Robert Coleman, there are basically only three types of stress: frustration, pressure and conflict. When we put it in these terms, we find it easier to understand, grasp and explain what stress is all about. Over the years while practicing psychotherapy and conducting stress management workshops, I found it useful and beneficial to clients and workshop participants to explain psychological stress in these terms.

You might say, "Okay, now I understand the simple terms when explaining what stress is, but I'm faced with some serious, monumental tasks." So you are! You might be facing for example, a job loss, foreclosure of your home, a divorce, an abusive father or mother, a home invasion, etc. Sure, these and many other instances are all very serious, threatening, dangerous or disastrous. These examples, along with the minor ones such as a crabby husband or wife, can affect us all in major ways. They all fit into one or more of the three kinds of stress pointed out. Stress is stress, no matter how minor or major it may be.

No matter the degree, type or duration of stress, stressors can deeply and permanently affect you. In other words, even the most incidental or minor stress event in your life might snowball into some deep depression, heightened anxiety or substance abuse related problem later on in your life. The stress might be a serious kind and affect us immediately, and in a life-changing manner. It seems we cannot escape the many stress-related events, incidences or experiences in life. Stress, in many cases, is related to a serious health issue or condition, and may affect you, your husband, wife, your children, parents, grandparents and friends. You may have a spouse with lupus, for instance, as in the case of my wife. You yourself might have a form of cancer, or a heart condition or diabetes. You might have an autistic child, one with cystic fibrosis. You might be living with an alcoholic husband or wife. The list goes on and on.

While it may matter to some if a health-related condition is acute vs. one that is chronic, others may be "stressed out" even with a child who has the flu. The strength and length of the health-related problem can affect people differently is the point being made here. One individual seems to deal fairly well with caring for a child with a chronic health condition, while another person "Goes to pieces" even when the child comes down with diarrhea over a 24-hr period. Whether a person has to cope with a loved one who has a life-threatening disease or simply has to attend to an elderly parent with a bad cold or bronchitis, it can and does affect each person differently.

Furthermore, it does not seem to matter if a person has only a high school education or a PhD; he or she is hit with minor or serious stress-related situations, events or experiences. Stress does not care whether a person is poor or rich. It may hit the person when he or she least expects it. It can impact one or more individuals in a family or in a circle of friends. Take for example when a family member or friend loses a job. The impact on the entire family group can be enormous. The spouse becomes worried as may the children, and each can feel pressured to do something about it. As time goes on, the spouse or the children might wonder why dad or mom can't seem to find a steady job. They worry about what other kids or people might think. They may hold their inner thoughts and worries inside but outside they may react very defensively to comments made by others. They may take their anger and frustration out on other family members or on close friends.

The children may start to perform poorly in school, get into fights on the playground or on the way home from school. You as an adult may begin to rationalize why they are in a bad mood, feel down in the dumps or lose interest in sports or other activities. "You'd feel or act the same way if you were in my shoes," may be the lament expressed.

Rationalization is the defense mechanism of choice for those using rational or socially acceptable explanations for why they act inappropriately as a means to covering up the true reasons or motivations behind the behavior. For example, if you raise your voice in a group or classroom because of frustration over not being heard or accepted by others, you may be seen as one who is normally quiet but simply wanted to have their opinion heard. In reality, you raised your voice, or even uttered a few swear words, because you are frustrated with being ignored by others or perhaps more importantly, you are frustrated because of the unemployed family member at home and the worries that situation presents.

To cover up your possible embarrassment, you do or say things that may be irrational or uncharacteristic. Then you make socially acceptable excuses for the irrational behavior later. For example, when a person goes to work after leaving the unemployed husband or wife at home, he or she may become very loud and angry when trying to make a point at a sales meeting. Later, this person may tell a co-worker, "Joe always seems to criticize my opinions or comments," or "I wanted him and the other staff members to know that I have something important to contribute to the group." That may sound plausible and understandable to others, but the real reason for your raised voice or angry outbursts has more to do with the frustration and pressure you experience from living with an unemployed spouse.

In this case, the use of the defense mechanism "displacement" also comes into play. You are not only frustrated with the unemployed spouse, you are also feeling pressured to perform well at work. When you come home from work, you may "kick the dog" so to speak or yell at the kids. Why? It's because you allow yourself to take your anger and frustration out on others. It's a way of letting off steam or so you think. You are feeling stressed out and feel justified in using both the defense mechanisms of rationalization and displacement, but there is one other significant defense mechanism you may use and that is "projection." This is when you falsely assign your own unacceptable feelings, impulses or thoughts to others. The others could be other family members, in this case, the kids, or the family dog or it could be friends or society and/or politicians at large. In other words, you look for the cause of your own thoughts and feelings of frustration as being that of the "big bankers," corporate management, the President or anyone else you may believe is the cause for the economic downturn. You learn to "project" the blame for your financial problems on "them" or others in the community.

Before moving on in our discussion, I'd like to share with you an old joke about how the defense mechanism of, "projection," works:

A man goes to see a psychiatrist. The psychiatrist shows him an inkblot picture and asks the man, "What do you see here?"

The man says, "Sex."

The psychiatrist shows the man another inkblot picture and asks, "What do you see here?"

The man says, “Sex.”

Then, the psychiatrist shows the man another inkblot picture and asks, “What do you see here?”

The man says, “Sex.”

The psychiatrist then says, “That settles it, you definitely have a sex problem.”

The man says, “What do you mean? You’re the one with the dirty pictures!”

We have talked about the stress associated with job loss and it’s affects on the spouse in the house. What about the jobless person? Here again, the three kinds of stress enter into the picture. The person who is struggling to find gainful employment or another more lucrative, fulfilling job may experience not only pressure, but also frustration and conflict. This person may actually experience a “vicious cycle” when it comes to job hunting. He or she may feel excessive “pressure,” including time pressure, because of verbal demands placed upon them by the spouse. For example, “How come you can’t seem to find a decent job like Fred (or Sue) has?” or “It’s been two months since you last went to a job interview. What’s the problem? We’re having a hard time meeting our mortgage payment, so when is the next job interview scheduled.”

Then, there is the internal “frustration” faced by the jobless person. He or she knows there have been numerous calls made to potential employers and numerous interviews but still no real job offers. He or she has revised the resume repeatedly, and has done all the “right things” according to recruiters or other job hunting specialists, but still no real progress in the job search. Finally, there is the “conflict” experienced by the jobless person in that he or she seems to be in numerous arguments with the spouse or other family members over what constitutes a “good” job, instead of a “dead end” one that may pay poorly. The person may only seem to find occasional, part-time jobs, instead of more permanent employment.

The feeling of conflict can go deeper wherein the person could experience any or all of the three kinds of conflict: approach-approach conflict, approach-avoidance conflict or avoidance-avoidance conflict.

Here is what some consider a funny, quick example of the "approach-avoidance" thought: seeing your mother-in-law drive off a cliff in your new Cadillac.

Approach-approach conflict may be exemplified by a situation where a person has to decide between two different job prospects. One may pay well or another one has a better work schedule. Still, another situation may call for an approach-avoidance conflict feeling. Such as a person presented with a job that pays well but the hours are very bad and would be hard on the spouse and family. Another example, a supervisory type job prospect wherein the person is attracted to being in a prestigious, powerful role as a manager, but job related pressure and long hours may be too great for the person to really find long-term job satisfaction. Finally, there is the avoidance-avoidance situation whereby the jobless person is unhappy about the low-paying job offer and with the low status; he or she would be in. Similarly, the person hates the idea of working at a convenience store or at a job requiring a long commute.

You can see how the jobless person feels all three stressors, the pressure starts and builds, followed by even more time-related pressure, followed by major feelings of frustration and inner turmoil, followed by verbal or behavioral conflicts with people around them to the point where even loved ones don't want to be around the stressed-out individual.

The example of a jobless person facing a job-search represents a "major" stress point in life. Stress can be viewed from a "minor" stress-related situation, too. Recently there have been some press related stories about "egg hunts" in some states. It seems some parents in communities in a few states have been perceived as being "bad eggs" when it comes to Easter egg hunting activities. Reports of parents in these communities have been pressuring their little children to "fight" harder or "look harder" for more colored eggs to fill their baskets. As such, they have been prodding their young children to crawl under the ropes separating various age groups in order to beat the younger or older children to the "hidden" Easter eggs.

You might think, "What's the big deal? Let the kids experience some competition to get ahead in life." On the other hand, you might wonder what is driving or motivating these parents to make sure their children get more Easter eggs than the neighborhood kids. I know some may say, "This is a dog-eat-dog society we live in so why not teach your kids to be more aggressive?" Whatever happened to kids just being kids, having fun in the backyard, neighborhood park or church play area, enjoying a good old fashion Easter egg hunt on a nice, sunny afternoon? It seems there is enough stress in an adult's life so why put a child through some unnecessary stress at an early stage in life. What are we trying to teach children with an Easter egg hunt? Is it to be the "top" egg collector, to learn to get along with other kids their age or simply learn to enjoy the thrill of finding as many colored eggs you can to fill your basket? Some children in a highly competitive, if not combative, Easter egg hunt situation might feel a high degree of all three stressors. Frustration with not finding enough Easter eggs to satisfy mom or dad, pressure to be "number one" when it comes to egg hunting activities, conflict with other kids the same age or with older kids who seem to get all the egg hunting "breaks."

Given the numerous, sometime chaotic Easter egg hunting events in some communities recently, the events themselves have been called off. When that happens, no one "wins" and the children become short-changed, losing out on what could be a wholesome, fun-filled social activity. This "minor" stress-related activity is just one example of how we may allow stress to creep into our lives without even noticing or expecting it. Stress may be in any individual's life or in any community, large or small. It may hit us when we least expect it and be devastating to individuals, families and the community at large.

Stress is so all encompassing that it can affect the person biologically, psychologically, socially and it can tear apart families and societies. It seems stress can impact us internally and externally by affecting our hormones, how we think and feel about life, and it can lead to destructive tendencies on the part of individuals and groups in society. As we have seen, stress can come in the name of joblessness, divorce, medical ailments and in societal breakdown. Stress can impact the lives of soldiers in Afghanistan, the families at home or even the Army reservists who do not know when a "shipment" to a war zone will come. Someone raped or victimized by child abuse can obviously experience stress. Stress can be experienced by children from broken homes or from growing up in a homeless family.

At the opposite end, a family can experience stress on vacation when parents and children argue about what vacation spots to visit next. Similarly, stress felt by a parent can make them anxious to get home to his or her loved ones after experiencing weather-related airport delays. Stress can be felt by a person feeling rushed to get through the grocery store line so he or she can get home in time to cook dinner before the nightly news comes on.

Here is another example. A man comes home from work after driving a long distance from a job meeting in another town. He has just spent two extra hours on the road in a long line of traffic due to an accident. In fact, he himself almost was rear-ended by a car following too closely. He comes home feeling tensed up and exhausted. One of the first things his wife says is, "Hey honey, our two kids and I have been talking about driving to the beach this week-end. What do you say to that idea?" You can only imagine what this stressed, tensed-up man is thinking and how he might react to this wife's suggestion at this moment.

As you can see by these examples, stress strikes all of us at any time in our lives and in practically any life circumstance or situation. It can hit us when we're most vulnerable and least expect it. Stress seems to be a natural part of human existence and no matter how hard we may try it seems we cannot escape its grip on our lives. Ask anyone if stress has been experienced in his or her life and the answer will inevitably be,"yes" and on numerous occasions. The next question will be, "What can you do about reducing stress in your life?"

Chapter 2

Dealing with Everyday Stress

Now that we have an idea of what stress is, what can we do about it? Stress has been a part of civilization from the beginning of time. Historians, philosophers and writers of various backgrounds all mentioned the pressures, frustrations and conflicts over the centuries. I want to mention one Greek philosopher in particular who knew how to deal with stress. Epictetus was a stoic who in the first century AD said, "Men are disturbed not by things, but by the view which they take of them." Such a thought provoking statement has made sense to me and to many clients in my career. In essence, what Epictetus was saying is, "It's not what happens to you or what someone says to you that matters, it's how you look at it or how you feel about it."

The late psychologist Albert Ellis in his book, "A New Guide to Rational Living" mentions this philosophical statement. It is the basis for Rational-Emotive Behavior Therapy (REBT). It gives people facing many of life's struggles hope and the opportunity to change their thinking about problems. Believe it or not, people can learn to live a more rational life instead of succumbing to erratic, irrational feelings and behavior. Without getting into the technical aspects of REBT, the basic premise is one that allows the individual to choose between the irrational and rational thoughts. For example, if you are feeling pressured to complete a work task within a certain deadline, you can think, "This is terrible. I'll never get this assignment in on time and I may get fired if I don't," or "This is a difficult assignment to complete in such short notice, but I'll just try and do the best I can, and hope the boss understands my time constraints."

One looks at the situation from an irrational point of view while another person may view the same situation in a more rational light. If the irrational person continues using such catastrophic terms as "terrible," "awful," "impossible," etc., he or she will feel intense anxiety or depression. Why? The thoughts are irrational and therefore negative; they will lead to feelings of distress and hopelessness. On the other hand, the more rational thinking person views the situation as "challenging," "exciting," "interesting," and even "self-fulfilling." As a result, the feelings are then of hopefulness, excitement and enthusiasm.

Here's another example of how individuals view the same event or in this example, a newscast in vastly different ways. Let's say a family is watching a news telecast about a flesh-eating disease (an event that actually occurred several years ago). After seeing the graphic pictures of some victims with large lesions on their skin, and after hearing about how the disease has affected many people with compromised auto-immune systems, each family members comes away with differing points of view on the subject.

The father may think, "Hey, this will be good for my stock in the "X" pharmaceutical company since they've been investing loads of money in research for a cure."

The mother may think, "Such disgusting report is being broadcast to frighten people into thinking they might catch this horrible disease."

The grandfather might think, "Gee, they never had such weird diseases when we were kids."

The teenage son might think, "Wow, this will be a good,

gross topic for me to write on for my biology paper."

The young daughter may think, "I can't wait to tell my friends about this 'thing' that's going around."

What's the point being made here? While this family was exposed to the same news broadcast and network discussion, each one forms a different perspective about the subject. Is it a particular subject matter that gets people down, anxious or even depressed; or is it the way one looks at the subject at hand? If it were the event, situation or a person's comments that affect how we think about it, everyone would have the same or similar reaction or response to it.

I am not saying unpleasant or even catastrophic events in our environment are not bad. There are bad things that happen to people every day and yes, there are violent crimes, wars, pestilence, even starvation that affect people throughout the world. Each one of us has the opportunity to react in more favorable, rational and positive ways to circumstances.

This calls to mind an actual historical event that took place in a Nazi concentration camp during WWII. Viktor Frankl, a Viennese neurologist and psychiatrist survived the holocaust in a Nazi death camp by looking at his grim situation and environment with hope instead of despair. He concluded that even though he couldn't change the situation he was in and escape getting hit by the guard, he felt they could not control how he thought. His basic insight in looking at his situation differently led to his formation of the three basic tenets, which are found in his book, "Man's Search for Meaning." They are:

- Life has meaning under all circumstances, even the most miserable one.
- Our main motivation for living is our will to find meaning in life.
- We have freedom to find meaning in what we do and what we experience, or at least in the stand we take

when faced with a situation of unchangeable suffering.

In essence, Frankl is describing how we can "think" about the situation we find ourselves in from a more hopeful, life-fulfilling point of view. As long as we are alive, have conscious awareness of the events and situations we find ourselves in, we can "choose" to think differently. Parents, other adult family members and teachers may teach us to react to certain events or situations in negative ways. We have always and still do as adults have the potential to respond more positively. I am not casting blame on significant others in our lives when we are growing up. I'm simply saying others may expose us to negative, ill-tempered reactions to circumstances and we can override their undue influence by looking inward to our own thought processes.

When we do, we realize we can notice and govern our habitual negative thoughts and decide to let those harmful thoughts go. For example, while most people can be bothered, upset and defensive if a friend or family member says something negative or critical about them, others seem to "blow it off." Why is that? It is true some people are just more "sensitive" by nature or temperament, and therefore, find it difficult to dismiss critical remarks by others. Even if you fall into this category, you have the capacity to view disparaging remarks by changing your thinking about them. You might allow yourself to be "hurt" by negative comments from others, but you can learn to let your thoughts about the comments go.

Easier said than done you might say. You might ask, "Just how do I let my thoughts and feelings go when a good friend says critical things about me?" What I have told people faced with this kind of situation is to simply take a deep breath, notice or see your thoughts about the negative comment as though you were watching a movie – just step back and see yourself as a viewer of the movie. In that way, you do not see yourself as being part of the movie. Another way I have told clients and others in the past is to have them view their thoughts as though they were part of a railroad train. Simply notice one or more train cars being old or dilapidated and watch them go by. Then, look over to some of the other train cars and see they are newer, brighter and more appealing. By using this technique, you might be surprised how you feel less angry, upset and let down by the negative comments made by others.

The upshot is you may never be completely free of stress associated with other people and their possible negative opinions. You can put yourself back in control of *your own* thoughts and feelings. In other words, by taking a step back and letting your thoughts about the situation or other people go away on their own, you begin to find inner peace and tranquility.

These suggestions on how to deal with your stress are only suggestions. You may find other ways of coping with stress. For example, you might take up yoga, meditation, relaxation exercises or rely heavily on anti-anxiety or anti-depressive medications. I will suggest other approaches to use in other chapters in this book. For now, I want to emphasize the importance of our thinking and the role negative thoughts play in feeling stressed.

The one thing we humans have in common is we are always thinking. You can't escape it. We are alive and conscious about ourselves and our environments, our brains continually process our thoughts. Even though we cannot turn our thoughts off, we can "catch" ourselves falling into the negative thinking trap. When we do, notice you are in control and you alone can do something about the thoughts going on in your head.

Whenever I find myself dwelling on some negative comment made by another person, I simply relax, notice my thoughts about the person or his or her comments and let them go. I find my next thought or thoughts are more pleasant, satisfying or even uplifting. Sure, it can be difficult to replace our negative thoughts with more positive ones, but it seems easier to do so if we don't fight with our thoughts or try so hard to let the negative ones flow away. It's like trying to remember a person's name or the name of some movie. The more you try and remember the name or work hard at it, the more difficult and time consuming it can be to do so. Instead, if we allow ourselves simply to "incubate" the inner command to identify a name, nature takes its course. In other words, if we "forget" about trying to recall a name, we will actually remember the name within a few minutes. It's funny how our minds work. We sometimes try too hard to change or correct things. It may be better to wait for the "correct answer" to surface in our brains.

This brings us to the discussion of control, specifically "locus of control," a theory developed by Jullian Rotter. According to Rotter[1], the basic premise is there are two kinds of control humans have by nature, "internal" control or "external" control. While everyone has both types of control within their personality make-up, some use "internal" control more. With internal locus of control, a person believes his or her's own actions lead to desired outcomes and accomplishments in life. On the other hand, a person with external locus of control believes things happen to them from the outside. The outcomes in his or her life are due to chance, fate or powerful others in society. They do not believe they have any voice or say in what happens to their lives.

You can find out what type of locus of control you have, and to what degree, by visiting website similarminds.com. Go to the "personality test" category and choose the "locus of control" item. This particular personality "test" is not fool proof. It can help you gain some insight into how you perceive yourself and the world around you. You are aware of how some people think when they make mistakes or fail to meet their goals in life. They might think, "I'm just a victim of bad luck," or "Others seem to always get the breaks in life." They have a "poor me" victim mentality with little choice in how things turn out for them.

If we return to the example of a jobless person, he or she

might think the cards are stacked against them. They might think, "I don't have the skills others seem to have in finding a good job," or "It takes pull to get a job" as though they have little choice in the matter. On the other hand, a person with a high degree of "internal locus of control" might believe it's up to them to find a suitable job. He or she feels self-confident and hopeful in the job search. They feel they know their strengths and weaknesses. They see certain career-related skills within themselves that will eventually lead to a satisfactory job. They may also realize the job hunt is not easy and job openings are driven by a weak economy. Still, this does not stop them from coming up with a sound job search plan and the willingness to put a full-time effort into the job search.

If you concluded you are a person who believes you possess a high degree of "external locus of control," you can change your thinking about outcomes in your life. You can begin to realize it's not all due to "bad luck," chance circumstances beyond your control or to others with more power, money and prestige. You have the ability to transform your life and to find happiness with greater satisfaction in your life. It's once again a matter of noticing your negative thinking, perhaps about the lack of good, paying jobs if you're in the job hunt. Allow yourself the chance to approach the job hunt with a greater degree of confidence and determination. In effect, you develop a "can do" attitude in your job search activities. You can reduce the impact of not finding a decent job and its stress related feelings (i.e., feelings of frustration, pressure and conflict). You can refuse to let the lack of job leads or rejections by prospective employers get you down.

You will notice some negative thoughts about the process (e.g., feeling no one will ever hire you, for whatever reason). Instead, tell yourself you have a good chance of acquiring a good job. You will put more planning into the job search activity, but you will also put aside some time for your spouse, family and yourself. In other words, you can balance your time between job search activity and personal endeavors. In that way, you will find more satisfaction while sending out resumes, making phone calls and going on job interviews. Why is this the case? You learn to relate to your previously negative thoughts about the job search in a more positive, constructive fashion.

I realize you may not be able to do it all alone. Life and in this case, a job search, can be less stressful if you are able to set aside time to talk to others. Let your spouse or close friends know about how frustrating the job search has been, with no real job prospects on the horizon. You could also join a "job club" or community support group to help you cope more effectively with the job search. Others can be instrumental in coming up with names, contacts, suggestions and advice on how to improve the job search endeavor.

There are always different ways to look at things. Stress is unavoidable, but you hold the keys to better coping mechanisms. You can change your outlook on life and on how you relate to the stressors in life. Check your negative thoughts at the door when returning home after a hard "hitting the pavement" job search.

I remember telling some clients to have a "box" in the garage or doorway to write down the negative thoughts they may have during the day, or to jot down some of the "bad" things that happened to them that day. They then are to place those little pieces of paper with the negative items into the "box" before they enter their homes. In this way, they relate to their significant others in positive ways without, perhaps, taking their anger or frustration out on them. Later in the evening, they might find themselves dwelling once again on the negative thoughts and things they placed in the box. When they do, they simply notice they're just "thoughts'"and the particular negative events or difficult people they had to deal with earlier in the day are not with them now. They or the events are not "real." Only their thoughts about them are real, at least to them. In that way, they may find it easier to "live and let go."

What you have read about stress is that it does exist, but you play a major role in how intense, frequent or impacting the stressors in your life can be. How we think can control a great deal of the effects stress has on our bodies and minds. Life can be challenging, taxing and very difficult at times, but you can rise above the occasion and view the stressors from a different vantage point.

Chapter 3

Give It some Thought

We talked about how it's a good idea to notice our thoughts and simply let them go. You might ask, "How do I solve a real life problem, like a job loss if all I do is just dismiss my thoughts about it?" That is a great question! I'm not suggesting you treat all your thoughts lightly or as if they're not important to you. Many of our thoughts are very important to us. How are you going to solve problems if all you do is worry, obsess and let them eat you up inside, or control your life?

When it comes to dealing with your problems by "thinking" about them, there is a rational way to address them. Let me point out an example of how our minds work. Let's say I am visiting with you in a relaxed setting, say a restaurant. You and I are sitting there, chit chatting about the day's events, what our kids are doing, etc. I ask, "Did you ask your boss for a pay raise like you said you were going to do the other day?" Your anxiety level goes up because the first thing you think about or visualize is facing a boss who is not normally an easy going person. You think, "Oh my God, I have to meet with my boss this afternoon about the Smith project and I have to bring up the fact I haven't had a raise in a year." Your heart starts pounding, your stomach is churning and you start to sweat in front of me. You really don't want to lose your appetite for lunch with me, so you quickly change the subject. When you start talking about your son, for instance, you feel excited and eager.

What changed about your inner feelings? You went from a feeling of anxiety to one of fun-filled excitement. You and I are still at a restaurant. You are not at work facing your boss about a pay raise at this time. The only thing that has changed is your thinking. If I had changed the subject from your work to your recreational interests, you would still feel the change in emotions. It is your emotions and mood changing in response to a thought about a situation. The event is the same, namely the relaxing restaurant social engagement we are in. It's the way our thoughts relate to the topic of discussion making the difference on how we are feeling at a given moment. The feelings may vary from anger or anxiety to joy and excitement just by flipping a switch inside our heads with our thoughts.

Now, just because we changed topics of discussion, the problem of having to ask an aggressive or "not-so-easy to get along with" boss about a raise is still there. It's not going away, nor your thoughts about the situation. You may find yourself thinking about the upcoming meeting with your boss later on in the day or at home while eating dinner with your spouse. Your loved one may ask, "Honey, what's wrong? You are so quiet tonight. Is something bothering you because you don't seem to be your usual, talkative self?" You may even begin cursing your job and all the pressures, big and small that you have to deal with every day. You may end up ruminating about your job and about how you deserve a pay raise. You may feel dread, uneasiness, even a sense of fear about your boss and the job. What will you do? Do you discuss your feelings with your mate or do you simply ignore your thinking about the job and start talking about "baseball?"

Remember, the problem is not going away. Your spouse believes in you and your work-related abilities. He or she may back you up in your desire to "confront" your boss about a much needed, deserved pay raise. When do you talk about it and how do you get up the courage and actually ask for the raise?

This is a good time for me to discuss problem solving and our thinking about the problems at hand. We can't help it when our thoughts about this problem or other problems "pop" into our heads. They just enter our conscious minds out of the blue. We humans all have the capacity to "think" and it seems we are constantly thinking about something. Often without us realizing it, we are bombarded with random thoughts that come and go.

We humans are blessed with two, yes two, kinds of thinking referred to as "process thinking" and "free-flow thinking." They are actually two different modes of thought recognition. According to Richard Carlson and Joseph Bailey, in their book, "Slowing Down to the Speed of Life" there are "differences between the free-flowing mode and the processing mode:

FREE-FLOWING MODE	PROCESSING MODE
Easy	Effortful
Passive	Active
Automatic	Contrived
Nonlinear	Linear
Deeper feelings	Conditional emotions
Uses memory selectively	Memory based and memory bound
Creative	Habitual
Spontaneous	Predictable
Big picture	Details
Forest	Trees
Vision	Tasks
Inspired	Scripted

Thought recognition is the key to slowing down and shifting gears. When we pause and reflect, our free-flowing mode takes over and guides us to the next step. It is our built-in automatic pilot; the wisdom that allows us to know the difference between the two modes and to know which one is called for at any given moment. When we can recognize our thinking, the next step will seem obvious—whether to put the issue on the back burner, to analyze it some more, to seek out more information or simply do nothing. This capacity to recognize our thoughts, with practice, becomes automatic and our mode of thinking changes from second to second.

As you see, we have a choice to make when thoughts about problems come into our minds. I need to point out once again, it's not the problem that is the problem, but our thoughts about the problem. Let's take another look at the pay raise issue. It doesn't matter if the thought about the problem enters your mind while you and I are having lunch at a nice restaurant, or if it bothers you while having dinner at home with your spouse. You have the choice of either dealing with the problem through discussion at the time it enters your head or to simply put it on the back burner. You can use either the "free-flowing" mode or the "processing mode" of thinking at any time. If you're not in a particularly good mood at our luncheon meeting, or while at home having dinner with your mate, then you might want to leave the problem for another time to deal with it. On the other hand, if you are in a good mood, you may want to look for advice on how to handle the uptight boss. Similarly, when relaxing at home over a fine dinner with your spouse, you may decide to talk about it and entertain his or her opinion on how and when to discuss the pay raise with your "difficult" boss.

Another route is to do nothing about the problem and simply wait for a time when the economy or your company business improves before discussing a pay raise. Still another way, using "free-flowing" mode is simply wait until a possible solution "pops" into your head. This is referred to as an "Ah ha, I have it" moment. It may occur to you that your boss is usually in a good mood on Friday mornings. He or she has been receptive to good job-related ideas at that time. You may decide to discuss the matter then in an open, positive manner.

Give some thought to a given problem or situation. You don't have to think serious, hard thoughts and come up with a solution just because the thought enters your mind at a given moment. You can let the thought "incubate" so a naturally occurring answer comes to mind.

Another example of how to use free flow thinking is when, let's say you are the manager of a large retail department store. One day, you receive an irate letter from a regular customer about the way he or she was treated by one of your employees.

This customer complains the employee was, "...rude, fat and obnoxious." You might wonder why anyone in today's world would be offended by a person being seen as fat. Why would any customer single out the description of "fat" in addition to other critical remarks? Maybe the customer has a weight problem and is projecting blame or finding fault with others because of her own problem.

Regardless, you as a manager and one who cares about customers and employees are feeling "pressured" to act on this complaint. While reading her letter, you are faced with a dilemma. Do you take the time from your very busy schedule to respond to the letter or choose to take some other route? You know you need to "give it some thought" and act on the complaint. But, how and when to act?

Maybe an assistant manager may even tell you he or she has received several complaints about this particular employee recently and wants to know, "What are you going to do about this?" Now, you have two problems to deal with, the disgruntled customer and a seemingly problematic clerk. Additionally, you have a problem with a "frustrated" assistant manager.

Your choice now is to use either your free-flowing mode or the processing mode of thinking. Either you can sit down at your desk and write a letter to the customer, then confront the clerk about the problem, or you can put the problem(s) on the "back burner." Here, once again, I want to emphasize that the problem is not the problem, but your reaction to it could be the problem. Your response to the problem could even make the problem worse. In other words, if you act defensively to the customer complaint and go off "half-cocked," you might write an angry response to the letter. If you did this, the customer might write a scathing, critical editorial in the local newspaper about you and your store. Furthermore, if you were to issue a sharp verbal reprimand to the clerk, you may compound the problem even further. Your employee might become defensive and decide to take her "case" to human resources or even go so far as to file some kind of age or other discrimination suit against you. If you don't act rationally and with sound solutions, it is possible things could mushroom from a mundane issue to serious problems down the road.

When faced with this dual-problematic situation, you may decide to put your response off until another time or later in the week. By using the "free-flow" thought process, you tell your associate, the assistant manager, you are going to go to lunch. The associate might say, "What? Are you going to ignore this situation? Especially, since I have to supervise this employee and put up with the complaints that are coming in?" In response, you might say, "I'm not going to ignore this situation, but I don't feel this is the right time for me to act. I need to 'think' about this for a while. Be patient and give me some time." You see how this approach may help to calm things down for a while so cooler heads will prevail?

Later in the week, when you are in a good mood and not pressed for time, you decide to sit down and write a nice, positive letter to the irate customer. In it, you might thank her for her letter and apologize for the treatment she received by the employee. You might tell her how you and the company have always felt a sense of pride for having good customer relations and for providing top quality products to the community. Your letter may even point out that the customer is number one and that it is the company policy to try and make the customer feel special when shopping at your store. You then tell the customer you'll take her complaint very seriously and intend to discuss the need for good, quality customer relations with this employee and all the other employees. You end the letter by telling her how much you appreciate her bringing this matter to your attention, and you include a $5.00 gift certificate.

Which approach do you think will garner positive feelings on the part of the customer? One where she receives an angry defensive letter or where she receives a positive, constructive response from a store manager that values her input? In this case, the latter approach would not have been possible had you decided to put everything else off and deal with the matter then and there. Now, for the second problem at hand, the employee who treated the customer poorly, which is also a "stressor" for your assistant manager. You decide to call a meeting with the employee and her supervisor. In the meeting, you ask the employee for her "side of the story" then proceed to tell her you expect her to show kindness and respect for all customers. You may even compliment her on how efficient she has been in processing customers through the line in a timely fashion.

The more positive and constructive approach will help the employee see the need for change on her part, but also realize she has some good skills as a checkout clerk. This approach, like the one you used in response to the angry customer, will lead to a better outcome as far as quality workmanship is concerned. Finally, with this case in mind, you may decide to address all employees via a store-wide meeting or employee workshop. You would be reinforcing the need for all employees to be more conscientious in dealing with any customer, including the "difficult customers."

At such a meeting or workshop, you might emphasize the need for improving manners. How many times have you approached a store clerk or restaurant greeter with a question only to hear, "What?" or "Huh?" Such a situation recently happened to my wife and me at a local restaurant. We asked about being seated in a certain section with a booth. The waitress used the "What?" and "Huh?" routine. The next day, I sent an email to one of the chain restaurant vice presidents. We received an immediate reply of, "We are sorry that happened" and "We will bring up the subject of manners at this restaurant's next employee meeting. We are attaching a coupon for a free meal at this restaurant." Is that or is that not a great way to resolve customer issues? Since then, at subsequent visits to this restaurant my wife and I have noticed dramatic changes in the demeanor and tone of the responses by the waitresses.

I did not just "bitch" about the ill-mannered staff at this restaurant to friends or relatives, nor did I remain angry about the situation for days on end. At the time it happened, I did not get hostile or confrontational with the waitress or restaurant manager. I simply put the matter on the "back burner" and dealt with it later on when I was in a "free-flowing" state of mind at which time I wrote the message to corporate headquarters.

Back to the case of the irate customer and the positive way you handled it. You might say, "Get real, the customer could still feel 'offended' by having been treated in a glib, rude manner by a fat, obnoxious clerk." Yes, this particular customer might indeed be viewed as a "difficult customer." She may even be prejudiced about fat people and therefore view this particular employee with bias and even hatred. As nice as your approach may be with this customer, you may not be able to change her negative attitude. My father used to say, "All you can do is try your best," at whatever you try to do in life. Who can fault you for trying? Certainly, your employee can't complain (too much) about calling this matter to her attention. Similarly, your group of employees can't really criticize you for making them go through occasional "staff development" workshops.

As the old saying goes, "You can bring a horse to water, but you can't make him drink." That reminds me of an old joke:

How many psychologists does it take to change a light bulb?

One, but the bulb has to want to change.

With people, or in this case your employees, you can try to change them or make them improve their work performance, or improve on customer relations, but you can't always expect to be successful.

Does this mean you beat yourself up when things (or people) don't change, as you would like them to? NO! To avoid being stressed out over the possibility of little or no change on the part of your employees, you learn to accept both, employees and customers for what they are. They're human beings trying to work and shop in sometimes crowded conditions with time constraints and people who may not be easy to work or shop with. As a store manager, you learn to use free-flow thinking at times and process thinking at other times.

A final point, when deciding which thinking mode to use, use the following guideline: The "process mode" of thinking is best used when you need to be analytical, objective and clear-headed. The following examples come to mind: when driving your car, reading a road map or using your car's GPS system, when taking a test for a job or in a college course, or when doing your income taxes.

The "free-flowing" mode" of thinking is best used in the following examples: when trying to recall the name of a person, movie or book; when giving serious consideration to a big problem such as the example of the difficult customer; when trying to figure out how to improve communications with others; when faced with a job issue. It might seem some situations like considering a job or career change are very serious and complicated, and therefore, call for more "processing" of your thinking about the situation, but you could be in a better frame of mind feeling less pressure and frustration when you let the "free-flow" thought processes unfold. This lets your mind come up with reasonable, rational conclusions or solutions. In other words, the "process mode" weighs alternative job prospects and you might want to defer to the "free-flow" mode when you need to make final decisions about a job or career change. All sorts of good, quality conclusions and decisions come when you are in a more relaxed state of mind. The two thinking modes are always there for you. You must be aware of which mode would be best to use when faced with complicated, difficult problem-solving situations.

Chapter 4
Living in the Moment

Most of us have heard the comment, "Get back to the moment," referring to staying focused on what you are doing. This is much easier said than done. Thoughts about the past and future constantly bombard our minds. No matter where we are or what we are doing, we usually find our minds wondering to something that was said or done to us in the past. Similarly, we think about all we have to do later this evening, tomorrow or next week. We face continual distractions taking us away from our current activity, no matter how much excitement or fun it may be. It doesn't matter if what we are doing now is stressful, challenging, upsetting or enjoyable and pleasing. Our minds seem to be an open box to everything happening to us in the past or will happen in the future.

We humans are constantly thinking. That's part of our nature and nothing we do can change it, or so we believe! Even though we can't help ourselves and stop random thoughts from entering our heads, we can do something about them. We all have free will and choices to make. If something from the past enters our heads while driving, watching a TV show or movie, or even when discussing current events with others, we can choose to allow those past tense thoughts to become present tense thoughts or simply observe them for a second, then let them silently drift away. In other words, we can allow those thoughts to interrupt what we are doing "for a second" then turn our attention back to the event or activity at hand.

There are "outside" interruptions inconveniencing us at times when we are engaged in a work or recreational activity. For example, we may be at home playing cards, having dinner with friends or relatives when the doorbell or phone rings. Oh, no, not another telemarketer! Yes, these things do and have happened to all of us, seemingly at the most inconvenient times. What do we do? We can swear about the interruption, talk impatiently and rudely to the person at the door or on the telephone, or simply hear them out and respond in a polite, cordial manner. We can calmly end the conversation with the person and go back to entertaining our friends or to whatever else we may have been doing at the time.

I'm not as concerned about these so-called outside interruptions as I am with "inside" interruptions. I'm referring to when we are trying to work on a project or assignment at our job, doing a Google search, relaxing with a good novel or a movie. It need not be something at work or home when we find our minds thinking about the past or future. How many times have you and your family been on vacation, let's say at a nice ocean or lakefront, when the thought in your head or family conversation turns to another subject? For instance, while enjoying the time with our family on a bright, beautiful day on the beach, you or a family member might bring up something like, "Hey, let's go play miniature golf tonight," or "Why don't we go to the Smith's cottage on the Florida Keys next month?"

Instead of truly enjoying the moment, relaxing on the beautiful beach where you and your family are, your mind and the ensuing conversation takes you out of the moment and into some other future endeavor. There is nothing wrong with planning a future event or activity when a thought about it comes up at a time like this, but why not simply put it aside for another day? Take another similar situation where you and your family are sitting on the beach enjoying a beautiful sunset when a beach runner comes by and stops to talk to you. She says something like, "Boy, you think this sunset is something? You should have seen the sunsets I saw last year in Hawaii." Not only is this an interruption by an innocent bystander, but your mindful perception of the current sunset has turned to another possible sunset location. You may find yourself thinking something like, "I sure wish I had the time and money to take my family on a vacation to Hawaii." Once again, your attention turns from what could easily have been a moment of "peak" fulfillment to one of angst.

Aside from intervening thoughts taking us away from some fun-filled, enjoyable moments, we frequently find ourselves stressed about unsolicited negative events or experiences from the past. I'm talking about tragic events you experienced in the past, including child or sexual abuse, or having gone through living with an abusive spouse and subsequent divorce. You may have experienced what you consider "failure" in the past. Either way, these negative occurrences can certainly make our present lives miserable. How do you free yourself from these past, negative experiences?

As you know, you cannot change the things that have happened to you in the past, nor can you change the failures and mistakes you may have made. Once again, you can choose here-and-now how you relate to the thoughts about those traumatic or painful experiences. Even though you experienced great depression or anxiety over these past experiences and may have gone through extensive outpatient therapy or took psychotropic medications, you find yourself plagued by annoying, painful thoughts from time to time.

The question becomes, "How do I relate to those negative, sometimes terrifying thoughts so they don't stress me out so much or take away from enjoying life now?" For example, you may be married to a wonderful spouse, have three wonderful sons and have several beautiful grandchildren. You are enjoying your retirement years. However, from time to time, you find yourself dwelling or obsessing about another career route you should have taken. Perhaps, if you had, you would have more money in retirement and could live in a much bigger house in California, instead of a modest home in a mid-western state where the winters can be tough at times. You may think it was a mistake not pursuing a PhD, instead of just a Masters degree and could have had an enjoyable, self-fulfilled career as a full-time college professor. You may consider yourself a failure for not taking a different, more lucrative career path. In essence, you find yourself feeling empty, rejected and downright sorry for yourself.

What's the alternative? You can't turn back the clock and do your career all over again. You owe it to yourself, your loving companion, to your loving children and grandchildren, to learn to live and enjoy life in retirement. Here are some possible alternative thoughts one can consider. First, had you pursued a different career route, it may have included getting a PhD and university professorship, but you might not have met your devoted, loving, kind, sweet, caring and beautiful companion. Your children may never have been born. Furthermore, had you taken a different career path, maybe the experience and accompanying stress would have led to a divorce or some difficult family problems. Instead, you realize how well off you are. You have a blissful, harmonious relationship, instead of one filled with tension, strife and disharmony.

Who is to say if you would have been "better off" with another career. It all gets back to counting your blessings, appreciating what you do have and thinking about past failures and mistakes differently. What will it take to stop "beating yourself up" or "kicking yourself" for past failings? It will take a new look at your present thought processes.

When the negative thoughts of the past enter your mind to interfere with your present thinking, observe them as you would a scene in a movie. Instead of feeling tense, ill at ease or even "depressed" over the movie you're watching, you wait for a tranquil scene to show up. If you were to view your upsetting, disturbing thoughts from the standpoint of watching a movie, you would find it easier to let them go by. In other words, don't let yourself get "hung up" on your negative thoughts!

Those negative, sometimes traumatic events and experiences of the past did happen and they were "real" at the time. Presently, the thoughts about the past are not "real," they are not "events," only thoughts. Here, I need to talk briefly about feelings. The more you dwell on the negative thoughts about the past, the negative feelings of discord, depression and anxiety will surface and be associated with those thoughts. It seems the equation of human existence is one of: THOUGHTS = FEELINGS=MOODS.

Even our low moods are associated with thoughts. Moods are nothing more than feeling states lasting for minutes or months. A psychologist told me once he was in a "low" mood for two years. No matter who you are, no matter the career or profession, no matter what "type" of personality you are, bad or low moods can take hold of you. It seems sometimes, even when you try to change your thoughts from negative to positive ones, low moods persist. Moods are part of life. How you relate to them can make a difference. If you react with great alarm to your low mood or react in an angry, critical way toward another person who is in a low mood, the more difficult it may be to change that mood. Sometimes the best thing to do is simply look at it as a low mood you or another person is in, and to let it be. NO NEED FOR ACTION! In time, with patience on your part, you may see the mood lift on its own, without any direct intervention on your part. However, please note that if you or others are experiencing a significant degree of depression, or have suicidal thoughts, than referral to an appropriate mental health profession for treatment may be necessary.

When looking at the benefit of staying focused on the present moment, we can take a page from the sports world. Here is a good time to point out how sports figures, their coaches and sports psychologists view present moment thinking. There are highly successful sports figures who train themselves on staying focused during a sports event. Such sports figures might include NBA basketball stars of the past such as Michael Jordan, Magic Johnson and Larry Byrd. You also have NBA athletes like LeBron James and Kobe Bryant, along with NFL quarterback greats such as John Elway, Joe Montana and present-day quarterbacks like, Peyton Manning and Tom Brady. Present day major league pitchers such as Justin Verlander and Tim Lincecum also fit into this category.

The reason these and many other past or current athletes are so good, aside from their natural athletic ability, is the way they can stay in the moment when playing. They may have taught or trained themselves to "tune-out" all unnecessary stimuli and to focus on the task. They don't let distractions by the competing players, the noisy crowd, the whistle-blowing referees or the many complicated plays in the back of their minds control their focus and current thoughts. They don't let themselves think about past mistakes or where to have dinner. They simply "see" the target before them and make the big play.

If these high-powered athletes can stay focused when it counts, you can also learn to stay focused. You can enjoy your job, hobby, family and friends by learning to stay in the moment. Even when you find a friend or work associate bringing up other topics, events or experiences detracting from the current activity, you can steer them back to the present. You can say something like, "Well that's a good or important thing to bring up, but can we finish this task first?" The same goes for you when you are busy or engaged in your hobby. You can "catch" or notice those thoughts about other things and let them go. For instance, while focusing your DSL camera on a particular mountain or ocean view, you may think about doing a "shoot" at another location. Instead, telling yourself you can think about and plan the other "shoot" later tonight, back at the hotel room or house. Allow yourself the chance to truly enjoy the photos you are taking for your family album.

What happens if you planned to take same great photos today while at, let's say, a family outing or when taking a hike in the woods, but you wake up to a cloudy, rainy day. Today, I find myself in such a situation. It is raining heavily and appears to be a day-long rain. Do I complain about it? NO! Instead, I am finding personal satisfaction, enjoyment, even comfort in staying home and writing this chapter. In the course of my work experience as an outpatient therapist, I had many clients complain about cloudy, rainy days in their lives. They found themselves feeling "antsy" or even "depressed" having to stay home during a rainy day. Many of my clients and people in general have serious problems in "coping" with cloudy, rainy weather. Many mental health experts and the media make a great deal out of S.A.D, "Seasonal Affect Disorder." Some construe this as a true mental disease. Whether or not you are plagued by this problem, whatever the cause, hormones, your genes, etc., you can learn to relate differently to your low mood due to rainy weather. You don't have to be miserable living under a "dark cloud."

I, don't feel I am a victim of S.A.D and do enjoy occasional rainy days. Looking out the window and seeing the low, dark clouds, seeing and smelling the rain, actually gives me comfort and makes me feel relaxed and at one with myself. You might think I'm crazy for feeling this way, but many people do. Even the happiness, guru, the late Richard Carlson in his book, "What About the Big Stuff?" points out he has a good feeling and feels relaxed when it rains. He does point out, however, that he knows many people who moved to Oregon where it rains a lot, only to be so displeased with the weather they end up moving back to sunny California. It's all in how you look at it. If you expect to feel down and depressed because of the rainy weather, guess what, you will feel low. Even when faced with many rainy days in a row, you can look inward for a positive thought. You can do something constructive like read a book, listen to some good music, watch a DVD or talk to your family or friends. When I say, "inside," I'm not necessarily talking about inside the house or building, but inside your own mind. Try some relaxation techniques like taking a few moments to breathe in and out very slowly, followed by meditation or yoga. This may be a good time to clear your mind of "clutter," busy thoughts about things you need to do or should be doing. Just take the time to enjoy sitting peacefully, perhaps by a fireside, thinking pleasant, carefree thoughts. In effect, you will be relaxed and in the "present" state of mind.

Now, for a true present moment EXERCISE! While you are sitting comfortably, reading this book, take this time to do the following:

Close the Book
Close your Eyes
Take Three Deep Breaths
Notice your Breathing
Tell Yourself, "I am Relaxed."
Let Your Thoughts Come and Go

I hope that you will have some feeling of relaxation, comfort, peace of mind and a wholesome sense of oneness of life. If you can take even five to ten minutes every day or even an hour to relax, ease out the negative thoughts from your mind and let the free-thought process unfold, you can find tranquil peace of mind.

You will see you don't have to always be pondering the future or entertaining thoughts of the past. I want to emphasize while we cannot control the random thoughts popping into our head, seemingly out of the blue, we can catch ourselves moving away from the present moment, and gently and calmly let ourselves return to the present. It will become easier to do with practice. Many of us are victims of our own bad habits. We allow ourselves to be accustomed to thinking about the past or the future without even realizing it. Consequently, you become victimized by past events or experiences having nothing to do with today. You allow yourself to become anxiety-ridden, worried or obsessed with events or situations that might happen. This reminds me of what my loving mother told me once about worrying. She said, "Anticipation is greater than the realization." I don't know where she got that from, but it stuck with me all these years.

Even though you realize worrying can't change the future or the outcome of our endeavors, you, as I have done, still find yourself worrying. By doing so, you take yourself out of the present time. You worry excessively because of having gotten into the habit of worrying. Another reason you might worry is because of your inherited genes. I'm referring to certain types of anxiety we can inherit. Even if you are prone to worry, no matter the etiology or cause, you can minimize worrying time by noticing your worrisome thoughts and to simply allow them to vanish. When you do, you will find yourself getting back to and enjoying the moment.

Chapter 5

Walk it Off

Let us now turn to another subject near and dear to my heart and I mean that in both the figurative and literal sense. Most of us have heard of the expression, "Walk the talk." One of the things I am a firm believer in is exercise. There are many forms of physical exercise. With today's focus on the country's weight gain epidemic, it is important to find time for some form of physical activity, anything from neighborhood basketball, golf, swimming, running, hiking, biking, soccer, weight lifting or other gymnastics.

There is one type of physical activity I have always been fond of and that is WALKING. The simple activity of walking, every day if possible, can do wonders for your stress level. When I mentioned that this subject is "dear to my heart," I mean just that. Back in 2007, I underwent open-heart surgery whereby I had an aortic "pig" valve installed. Prior to that, I had four back surgeries. When I asked the doctors if I could continue walking as a form of good physical activity, they said, "Sure, by all means." In taking their advice and in fulfilling my own need for some "outside" stress release mechanism, I walk and walk. I try to walk at least two to four miles every day. If I travel about 3.4 miles, it takes me a little over one hour to complete the journey.

Both my cardiologist and orthopedic back surgeon emphasize how walking can positively affect my breathing, strengthen the heart muscle and help maintain a regular heartbeat. As for my back, such exercise can help strengthen my vertebrae column. However, before I discuss this activity any further and before you take up a walking regimen, I strongly urge you to discuss your exercise plans with your physician.

What are some of the other benefits to walking? Like running or other forms of physical exercise, walking can get the "endorphins" going in the body. These biochemical corticosteroids are produced by the pituitary gland and the hypothalamus of the brain. While endorphins tend to surface in response to pain and are a lot of times associated with pain tolerance, they can also increase your level of "excitement." These naturally occurring endogenous opioids can help you "feel good." In general, walking is an exhilarating experience. It doesn't require any training or particular technique. It is only natural for humans, starting as children at a young age to stand up and walk.

I began writing this chapter on walking today, after taking a nice, medium fast-paced walk for over three miles. As I write this, it is a very nice late April spring day, with a pure blue sky, and a 10 – 15 mph northeast wind at my face. The air is clean, and listening to the singing of the birds, while seeing the deciduous trees blossom, and the evergreen spruce and hemlock trees flowing in the breeze gives me a feeling of JOY! It makes me feel at one with nature. Such harmony in life can be experienced by anyone if they only allow themselves the chance to do it. Walking, no matter the pace or distance can give anyone a feeling of elation.

You can become a "walker" if you're not already one. You can choose to walk with a companion or simply walk alone. You know the old song, "You'll never walk alone" that they usually play at graduation ceremonies? Well, it is comforting to know you have family members and friends who will walk with you from time to time and be there when you need them to help walk along side of you in life. I have enjoyed walking with my beloved wife over the years, including taking hikes when camping. I also enjoyed walking with my sons and grandchildren over the years, and I look forward to future walks with them.

There is also something to be said for walking alone, to experience a sense of solitude. While the word, "solitude" can have some negative connotations, such as the feeling of isolation and loneliness, it can also have positive ones. When alone, walking with God within His natural surroundings He created for us, we can let ourselves go and tap into our sense of spirituality. Being in touch with nature is so uplifting and fulfilling at times it can almost bring you to tears. When I mentioned about the effect of endorphins on our bodies, I was not only referring to what has commonly been called a "runner's high" but also to what I call a "walker's high." It is similar in its effects, but I think walking goes one-step further. It helps you to relax and enjoy the moment. Furthermore, it allows you to free yourself of troubling thoughts.

Solitude has both negative and positive aspects to it. For instance, adolescents many times abhor solitude. They dislike being alone. They may feel lonely and unhappy if not with others. They need to be with their friends. As they become adults, they see the benefit of solitude as a way to bring balance to their lives. Yes, it's true anyone, no matter the age, if faced with too much solitude like a prisoner in solitary confinement, could face major depression. What I'm talking about is finding balance between social time and being with others, and finding time for privacy, just being alone. You can find quiet time not just being home alone in your living room listening to some good music on your iPod, but also on the walking or hiking trail. Notice the photo I took on the walking trails I use near my home. It is a fairly wide winding road, filled with trees, hills and some open sky. As you see from the photo, it is truly breathtaking and its environment beckons one to walk and enjoy the fruits of its surroundings.

Such a walk in an open space helps create a feeling of solitude. It seems Spiritual Guru Buddha attained a sense of enlightenment with meditation, welcomed solitude. It is assumed Jesus Christ and many Bible figures, including Moses, enjoyed solitude on occasion, to pray and reflect on life and nature. I want to emphasize while solitude is usually associated with being inactive, i.e., quiet and still, it can be found or take place during a leisurely walk in the woods.

In general, one of the major benefits to the art of walking is relief from stress. As we have discussed, stress make us ornery, tense, angry and just plain 'ole difficult to be around. When that happens, you can simply tell the person you're with, "I'm going for a walk." Yes, walk off whatever may be troubling you, making you feel down in the dumps. Walking can be a useful tool to use to ward off stressful feelings. It will give you a chance to clear your mind and if in a confrontational situation with another person, a chance to get out and clear the air. When you return from your long walk, you find a deep sense of calmness, fulfillment and a general feeling that life is good.

I mentioned how many adolescents detest solitude at times. When they do not allow themselves the opportunity to be alone with their own thoughts, they might be short changing themselves when it comes to creativity. They need to be creative in school and need to demonstrate some creative ideas around friends and classmates. This is very important at a young age. It's also important for grown adults who want to be more creative in their careers. Here again, walking can be the answer. It can allow the person who is out walking to take advantage of the time for free-flowing mode thinking to unfold. You would be surprised at how many ideas and solutions you can come up with by taking a walk.

Most people would prefer to walk in nice warm, sunny weather. As you know that's not always possible. You can and many people do walk in the winter months when feasible. Even when it is relatively nice out during the winter, you still have to use common sense and caution to avoid unnecessary slipping or falling. Nevertheless, there are three other seasons to take frequent walks in, especially Spring and Fall. These can be very good times to experience inner joy and elation when you take in nature's beauty. Ah, the budding and the greening of the trees, the fresh, relatively warm spring days. In the Fall, just walk and smell the crisp, freshly fallen leaves and observe the fall colors at their peak.

For those of you who live in a one or two season state, well, enjoy the sometimes boring consistently beautiful, blue skies and warm weather when walking on a daily basis. The point of mentioning the effect of the seasons, no matter how many there are, is we are blessed with nature's abundance and beauty. Take the time out from your hectic, busy schedule and make it a habit to put in some walk time. You will be glad you did.

I mentioned the use of free-flowing mode thinking to come up with creative ideas. This mode of thinking can allow you to appreciate nature's beauty when walking. For instance, when in a free-flowing mode of thinking, you allow your senses to take in the sights and sounds of the birds around you. It's not necessary for you to be an ornithologist and use the "process mode" of thinking to try and identify types of birds when listening to their chirping. Similarly, you don't have to come up with names of birds you see along the trail. Just allow yourself to enjoy the beauty of the birds or other animals while strolling comfortably along the path. Walking is as easy or as difficult as you make it.

I realize walking can be difficult for some people struggling with a debilitating disease, illness or injury. As I mentioned before, my own wife has lupus and consequently has struggled with the many side effects medical problems associated with it (e.g., arthritis, chronic pain in the joints, etc). As a result, many people feel deprived of the opportunity to do something as simple as taking a casual walk. This is where loving, supportive partners can help or where community support groups can help. Undoubtedly, stress can enter into the picture. A person with acute or chronic medical conditions, including lupus or multiple sclerosis and other diseases, can feel devastated by the physical limitations imposed upon them. This is where family and friends can help make the medical problems a little less burdensome. For instance, a husband or wife can take the spouse with the medical problem on a walk with the use of a cane, walker or wheel chair. Both partners can take the time to enjoy the great outdoors and life itself. This is where love, support and patience can pay off. Let's suppose you have been in good health and enjoying daily walks. Then one day you twist your ankle or simply become bed ridden with the common flu. What do you do? You feel frustrated, perhaps or depressed because you are thwarted in your efforts to get your exercise in. Well, you can lay around feeling sorry for yourself. You could even take your frustrations out on others in the family by yelling at them, being impatient or even by taking it out on the family pet. On the other hand, you could stay in you favorite chair or lie in bed and take the opportunity to meditate. You could even take the time to fantasize or visualize walking along your favorite path, in the woods, along a hillside or along a beach. Yes, it is possible to experience similar good feelings through in vitro realization of a walk experienced in your mind.

In might take some getting used to and some practice sessions, but even though you may be temporarily laid-up, you can fantasize about the great, exhilarating walks you have had and bring the experiences to your conscious mind. Walking serves its purposes when you are actively engaged in it or when you are inactively apart from the activity. It's all the more important for you to make walking a regular part of your daily activity when you are in good health. Similarly, it behooves you to take advantage of good, decent weather while the sun shines so you can better appreciate such days when you are home and unable to walk.

When it is difficult or impossible for you to get outdoors to enjoy a walk with nature, there is a good alternative means of walking transportation, the TREADMILL. However, before you start using the treadmill or any other exercise equipment, the elliptical bike for instance, do consult with your physician or heart specialist.

Now, let's talk about the type of terrain and difficulty of a bike or walk path to use. Ideally with my having several back surgeries and all, I prefer a paved, relatively flat path to walk on. That may be construed by some as an easy trail but given the frequency and the amount of time I spend on the trails, that's good enough for me. You, on the other hand, depending on your age, general fitness and health, might choose a dirt trail with many curves and steep terrain. Regardless of the type of trail and degree of difficulty, I truly believe you will get a natural high in your walking routine.

Let's say instead of walking, you feel a need for a more rigorous workout. You may consider bike or walking trails with lots of medium to high grades of incline, but also community parks which have numerous climbing stairs. If you're in a metro location and want something like a long, paved trail, then I strongly suggest a scenic linear park with a nicely paved, tree lined trail.

Walking or hiking should be included in your daily exercise program, even include it as part of your vacation plans. Before you go, I urge you to check out the numerous listing of parks and greenways online. Whether you plan on vacationing or even moving to a particular state or geographical location, I suggest you do some online research about the parks and greenways in the area. For the reasons of stress reduction, spiritual uplift and physical exercise, walking is essential to good quality of life for you, your spouse and children.

To help you zero in on some possible great parks and greenways, I put together a partial list of some scenic, beautiful sites with super photos or video clips in various parts of the country that you may want to check out:

Paint Creek Trail, Oakland Co., Michigan
Bloomer Park, Rochester, Michigan
Fred G. Bond Metro Park, Cary, N.C.
Lake Johnson Park, Raleigh, NC
French Broad River Park, Asheville, NC
Venetian Waterway Park, Venice, FL
Oso Creek Trail, Mission Viejo, CA
Shell Ridge Open Space, Walnut Creek, CA
Iron Horse Regional Trail, Alameda Co., CA
Almaden Lake Park, San Jose, CA
Poudre River Trail, Fort Collins, CO
Spring Creek Trail, Fort Collins, CO

As a matter of fact, if you find yourself in a low mood and not able to get out of the house for whatever reason, just turn your computer on, visit one of many of such websites and sit back to enjoy sort of a travel log of a park trail. It will relax you as you admire the photos or the YouTube clips.

As you have been reading this chapter on walking, you might ask out of curiosity, "What started you on this walking kick?" Well, to make a long story short, it all started when I was a little boy. I remember doing a lot of walking with my father, brothers and older cousin. I have fond memories of walking with my father on a beautiful, crisp autumn evening (in October), pulling a little wagon filled with apples. The moon was bright and my father told me his usual stories. I felt truly blessed.

Chapter 6

Avoid Agitated Avenue - Choose Serenity Lane

We now come to what is the proverbial fork in the road. Here, I'm talking about choosing to live a life of agitation and chaos or one of peace and serenity. I realize as much as we might prefer it, we can't always drop everything and enter into a calm, tranquil state. It seems most people we know are constantly busy, doing something at work or at home with family obligations. The activity we find ourselves in may include running the kids to soccer, little league, band practice, ballet, football or basketball games, swimming classes, to a drama class or unfortunately, to the doctor.

We find ourselves busy in the garage, in the garden, in the kitchen preparing dinner, doing the laundry or fixing the kitchen sink. You name it and we are constantly on the go or taking care of unfinished business. In our modern day society, if you don't know anyone who is not busy with some type of activity, we wonder if they are just plain lazy, uninterested, sick or simply retired. What I am talking about in general is how stressed we have become. In seems the American society thrives on living a stressful existence. We seem to work longer hours and be involved in more social or family-related activity than our counterparts in other countries. In short, our jobs and our family lives seem to consume us.

What seems to be baffling is we feel good about ourselves when we are kept busy. In other words, we feel it is only normal to be stressed out. If you were to ask someone, "How are you doing?" They are apt to say, "I have been so busy that I don't have time for myself." It's as though they are bragging about their busy, stressed-filled lives. As a consequence, everyone seems to believe they're so stressed out that it affects their work life, their professions, their family life, their marriages, and of course, their own sanity.

Let's say you were to tell someone you relish the thought of finding a time for silence in your life, spend some time alone, feeling a sense of peace and joy. That person may say, "If I did that, I would have a nervous breakdown or go crazy." In other words, if you were able to take "Serenity Lane" in life when possible, other people would continue traveling along the "Agitated Avenue" of their lives. Choosing between these two roadways is not something that can come easily for many. It is possible to make the choice between these two roads in our busy lives.

We all know what it means to be busy but what is, serenity anyway? It simply means to be in a serene, peaceful state. It is a time frame whereby a person feels calm, tranquil and at ease with life. It's more than a time frame or a time when you are inactive. It's more a state of mind when you can be still, let go of unnecessary, even harmful and disturbing thoughts and simply be.

The person, who might experience a nervous breakdown, if they were to find themselves in an inactive, quiet time frame, may not believe it is possible to find a state of serenity. They may think it next to impossible, given our active, highly charged lives. That person believes he or she needs stimulation to find happiness and enjoyment in life. After all, what is life for and what are we on this earth for if it isn't to find excitement and thrills through constant activity?

We Americans thrive on the work ethic. We put in long hours at work, spend hours in traffic and increasingly take on more job-related responsibilities, and in many cases, work two jobs, to try and get ahead. After all, like the wealthy, former Governor of Massachusetts, Mitt Romney said, "What's wrong with success?" He, like many of his wealthy friends; knows hard work, good career planning and good financial investment-type planning has paid off. Even though Romney might be a part of the one percent of Americans, many in the other ninety-nine percent want to maintain high standard of middle class living and be able to retire in relative comfort.

Don't get me wrong, I'm very supportive of doing your best to get ahead in life, to be someone, be successful in your career endeavors and provide a satisfactory lifestyle for you and your family. This is where good, short and long-term goals for life and work come into play. We know money and job-related success does not come easily. We have to work at whatever we try to accomplish in life in order to reap its benefits. To live most of your life in the "Fast Lane" or on "Agitated Avenue" can take its toll on you. Even if you don't have a "Type A" personality, staying in the fast lane for too long a time can lead to serious physical, psychological and social problems, including marital discord and family dysfunction.

I'm not condemning living life in the fast lane or in an agitated state of being completely. Doing so on occasion can make for an interesting, exciting and stimulating existence. The problem comes from living way too long in a chaotic, restless, high-energy state. Once again, live a more balanced lifestyle. Try to spend some time in "Serenity Lane." This is when you can recharge your batteries and find peace, harmony and relaxation.

The question becomes one of how to find the time for relaxation and yourself. Well, to begin with, try saying the St. Francis, "Serenity Prayer:"

"God, grant me the serenity to accept the things I cannot

change, the courage to change the things I can, and the wisdom to know the difference."

This little, timeless prayer can provide you with almost immediate calmness and relaxation. Try to practice saying it when you feel tense, agitated, restless and anxious. You'll be surprised at the calming affect this prayer has on your psyche.

You can try using any number of relaxation techniques, meditation and yoga. One particular relaxation technique you can try is breathing slowly in and out, followed by tensing and relaxing your muscles. But probably the most important relaxation exercise is in the breathing. Notice your breathing. Start with taking in three deep breaths and then let them out slowly. Do this before trying to tense up and relax your different muscle groups.

Besides the breathing and muscle relaxation exercises, another very important way to relax is to listen to soft music, perhaps using your iPod or CD player. Spend at least a half hour to a full hour in a sitting or laying position, in a free-flowing mode of thought, absorbing the music, and letting your thoughts drift by endlessly and effortlessly. This may be the opportunity to recall pleasant memories from the past or to fantasize about being on the beach, in the mountains, by a soft sounding brook or watching a glorious sunset. Let your mind just wander.

I'd like to suggest several CDs I have found to be particularly beneficial in relaxation. You may very well fall asleep while listening to any one of these beautiful works of music. Just use the time to let those bothersome, troubling or fast-paced thoughts come and go.

"Sound Body, Sound Mind for healing," by Andrew Weil, MD
"Mozart for Meditation"
"Beethoven's Sixth Symphony" (The Pastorale)
"Brahms at Bedtime"
"Pachelbel Canon and Other Hits of the Baroque"

"Songs of Faith and Inspiration" by Robert Shaw Chorale
"Stephen Foster Song Book" by Robert Shaw Chorale

I'm not getting any kind of commission by trying to sell these recommended CDs, or musical selections for your iPod. I find them to be especially inspirational, uplifting and in some instances, faith based. For example, the Andrew Weil CD on meditation has a symphony of brain waive music, including the Mozart adagio from Concerto No. 3 and selections from Mahler, Bach and Brahms. As Dr. Weil mentions on his CD, "Sound is an effective, powerful instrument on the human nervous system." This CD is totally relaxing and I appreciate this being one of the best gifts I have ever received from my darling wife, Maureen.

Additionally, I strongly recommend the CD by the Robert Shaw Chorale, "Songs of Faith and Inspiration." This CD has such inspiring, uplifting selections as the two versions of, "Ave Maria" by Schubert and Bach, "Panis Angelicus," "Were You There?" and "Nearer, My God, To Thee." You may remember this last piece being played in one of the "Titanic" movies; I believe the 1953 release, very haunting to say the least.

Try this relaxation/meditation time daily or at least once per week. If you do, you will find life on "Serenity Lane" to be a nice way to live to balance out your more regular active time on you-know-what avenue. After listening to soft, even "heavenly" music for a few minutes at a time, you may come away feeling relaxed, refreshed and in a more tranquil frame of mind. This may do wonders for your mood and may even enhance your relationship with others.

At this point, one question you may be asking, "What happens if I can't seem to let go of some negative thoughts while trying to unwind, relax, and enjoy the soft, soothing music?" That is a good question. Let's suppose while sitting or laying down and listening to this soothing music a thought pops into your head about something in your life recently. Let's suppose you told a friend about some very personal things you feel is very private and secret. Your friend promised not to reveal it, but you find out he or she has betrayed your trust by telling another person. Consequently, you have increasingly been bothered by what has transpired. Lately, you feel angry, resentful and disappointed in your friend.

Since you allowed yourself to go into some periodic "thought attacks" about this incident, you have found it difficult to not only let go of the negative thoughts and feelings, but you have not been able to relax while in the company of others, and at home alone. You find your sleep has even been disturbed because of this event. What to do? For starters, whenever the negative thoughts enter your head, you can notice it is just a thought. While you can't change what has already occurred, you can change your thought about it.

When you are trying to relax and meditate, the negative thoughts about your friend creep back into your head—gently let that thought go by. Notice and appreciate the inspirational music, then let it lift your spirits up. If in a few minutes, the nagging, disturbing thoughts return, once again notice they're just thoughts, they can't harm you and allow yourself to let them come and go.

Just because you've given yourself permission to enter the relaxation or meditation exercise, your problem with the friend will still be there when the period is finished. Keep in mind what we have already discussed and you will be able to find a possible answer or solution to the problem at another time. Perhaps, when you are going about your normal, daily activity a more positive thought about what to do with your friend will enter your consciousness via the "free-flowing" mode of thinking.

In time as you learn to observe and let go of such negative thoughts, you will realize you can still find peace and harmony in life. Your happiness doesn't depend on what your friend says or does, or on what other people may think of you. What good does it do you to live your life filled with anger, resentment and hatred? Such an event, like many other unexpected, disturbing experiences can destroy us if we let them. This is all the more reason to take the time to enter a period of serenity to relax and meditate whenever feasible.

Now, let's talk a little about "quantity vs. quality." It seems when we live in the fast lane, ergo "Agitated Avenue," we tend to focus on getting ahead in life by acquiring many things or objects. We foolishly think if we can improve our purchasing power by earning more money and by buying more things, having more possessions, we will be happy.

It's the mentality of "if only" that may motivate you to try and improve your lifestyle by working yourself to death. As the old saying goes, "Money can't buy happiness." Look around you and see how many people are truly happier having acquired a new car, a bigger, newer house, moved to a better location, etc. Look how many sports figures, celebrities and other wealthy individuals are happy with their multi-million dollar mansions, fancy cars, expensive vacations and their overall luxurious lifestyles. Not many! As you know from media reports, they are often addicted to drugs and alcohol, divorced or in trouble with the law. Hardly a day goes by without a news report of some athlete or movie star being arrested for a DUI or for a domestic violence charge. Does that account for living a life in a fast-paced, chaotic, hectic, pressured-filled lane? Maybe it does.

Some people are of the opinion living a more serene life can be BORING. It may be if you haven't learned to do the things I have been suggesting. Living a relaxed life most of the time may be impossible. Therefore, plan to SWITCH back and forth between a highly charged, active life at times, followed by states of calmness and relaxation.

I want to reiterate, there is nothing wrong with trying to improve your lifestyle for your benefit as well as that of your loved ones. However, if we do not try to take some time off by engaging life in a more relaxed, down-to-earth fashion, we may end up burned out. It all gets back to the importance of finding balance in life, to stepping back and rejuvenating your energy level by living life more on Serenity Lane. You will find greater peace, harmony and fulfillment. Furthermore, to your surprise, you may be able to enhance both your mental health and your lifestyle in the process. Life on Serenity Lane can lead to greater freedom from stress and to a more rewarding life.

Chapter 7

Landscape Escape

This is a unique chapter especially designed for people who feel like they're caught up in a hectic, fast-paced lifestyle. Whether or not you are such a person, you may find comfort in slowing down your busy mind by reading the individually named passages and by looking at the accompanying beautiful landscape photos I have taken when relaxing.

Try to visualize yourself in these photos as though you are there, seeing nature's gifts as they unfold before your eyes. Never mind you may have already read parts of these passages in this book so far. They are presented again as thought-provoking passages of wisdom to reinforce their messages.

I have been an amateur photographer since I was a teenager. Over the years, I have taken thousands of pictures of people and of various landscapes. I choose these particular landscape photos because I believe they portray not only light and color, but also send messages of comfort, healing, serenity and feelings of peace and tranquility.

Sit back, relax and escape into the landscape of positive, uplifting words and beautiful pictures. Reflect on the individual passages of positive thoughts and absorb the portrayal of peaceful views of light and scenery.

ENJOY the JOURNEY!

Lake Charlevoix, Michigan

A. ATTITUDE

One's outlook on life is a reflection of his or her attitude.
The proverbial question has been and always will be:
"Is the glass half empty, or is it half full?"
It depends on <u>your</u> point of view.
We all have choices to make when faced with challenges or problems at home or at work.
From one moment to the next, we can choose to look at life or work through negative "filters," or through clear, positive "lenses."

B. THOUGHT

Whether or not you realize it, while at home or at work, you are just a thought away from happiness.
Negative thoughts are nothing more than passing thoughts.
When you handle the remote controller of the DVR player of

life, you can either hit the "pause" button and blow your negative thoughts out of proportion and dwell on them, or you can hit the "play" button and simply let those negative thoughts or scenes go.
So, why not sit back and simply observe or watch your negative *and* positive thoughts flow, as they run through the movie projector of your mind.

Walloon Lake, Michigan

C. FEELINGS

Our feelings are merely reflections of our thoughts.
If we are feeling low, sad, angry, or frustrated, at home or at work, it's usually because we are thinking negative or problematic thoughts.
On the other hand, if we are feeling happy or in good spirits, it's because we are thinking positive, pleasant, or enjoyable thoughts.
In effect, our negative feelings are like the "Check Engine" light on the dashboard of life. The feelings serve as warning

signals to pull-over, check your thoughts and either rest until the problem can be worked on another time or day, or call for more immediate help if overwhelmed or stressed.

When driving down the road of life, **listen to a positive feeling** as you enjoy the beauty of the roadside scenery.

D. DIFFERENCES

It is always better to view the other person's opinions, judgments, ideas, or critical remarks as just different points of view. The apparent differences between your thoughts and ideas, and those of others in your personal and work lives are simply separate realities.

In essence, how you and others look at things has more to do with merely different observations or thoughts than it does with who is right or wrong.

Relationships at home or at work would be much more loving and peaceful, and free of bickering, backbiting, arguments, or conflicts, if people would simply see each other's thoughts and opinions as just different ways of looking at things.

With this higher level of understanding of differences, people will find greater harmony and peace in their personal and work lives.

Lone Cypress Tree, Monterey Peninsula, California

E. PRESENT-MOMENT LIVING

We all have choices to make when it comes to living life in the moment. We can camp out with our memories of the past, hanging on to anger, resentment, or hopelessness when thinking about past experiences. Similarly, we can worry, be fearful or apprehensive about the future and what might happen to us or to our loved ones. Or, we can simply let the thoughts of the past or future go, and get back to enjoying the present. Yes, we can look out onto the horizon of life and see the beauty of life, human beings and other living creatures. Realize that we are all on this earth for only a short period of time. So why not take advantage of the time we have and live life as we experience it - in the here and now.

F. WISDOM

How many times have you tried to recall a person's name after seeing that person at a store or social event but just couldn't remember his or her name? Well, as you may have realized, the more we try to force a name recognition or recollection, the more mental blocking we seem to experience. Instead, if we simply put the desire to recall a person's name in the "incubator" of our minds, the more apt we are to have the person's name "pop up" in our consciousness. The same thing holds true for more serious, complex problem situations, relationship difficulties, work-related conflicts or issues, or other problems in life.

Simply put, wisdom knows what is the right thing for you to do in a given situation, event, or relationship.
In effect, wisdom provides common sense.

When we simply let go of worries, problems, or memories, realize that they are just harmless thoughts, and we are better able to see life more clearly. We are more likely to come up with solutions to problems we never thought possible. In essence, the more we try to figure out, or force a solution to a problem, the more difficult it becomes to see the "forest for the trees." But, when we put our problems on the back burner so to speak, let the negative thoughts flow through our minds, and let our natural wisdom do its job, the more likely we are to see alternatives or answers to difficult situations or problems.

Mt. Shasta, California

Harbor Springs, Michigan

G. INSIDE-OUT LIVING

Many people believe they feel sad, angry, frustrated, or happy because of all the influences on their lives, i.e., parents, schools, jobs, and relationships. But whatever a person is feeling is actually the result of his or her personal reality, their own train of thoughts at any particular moment. People think that their jobs, other people, or the circumstances they are in are the cause of stress in their lives.

In essence, there is only internal stress created by our own moment-to-moment thoughts. In other words, stress isn't something that happens to us from "out there." Actually, stress happens from the inside, within our own thinking. It all boils down to how we view or look at the outside influences on our lives. So, instead of hopping on a train of thoughts about how your boss, a co-worker, or your mate criticized you yesterday, you can simply let that train pass by your depot.

You can get back to enjoying the moment -watching a movie, reading a book, listening to music, or having an intimate dinner with your loved one, or engaging in quality time with your son or daughter, without dwelling on thoughts about what happened "out there." In essence, your momentary and daily experiences are created on the inside, by the power of your own thoughts. What a gift we were given!

Ashland, Oregon

H. PEACE & SERENITY

If you're feeling stressed at work or at home, give yourself a break and take a "time-out." Whenever you're feeling low, insecure, rejected, in a bad mood, or thinking negatively you face a fork in the road.

To continue on your journey, you can choose to take "Agitated Avenue" and get caught up in your own thoughts, or "tranquility trail," and just let the thoughts pass by. You don't have to try and figure out why you're feeling bad or filled with discontentment, nor do you have to blame others, your job, or your circumstances for your low mood.

Simply accept it as a passing mood or negative thought, realizing that "this too shall pass." You will then be able to tap into your natural state of mind with its inner peace and calm.

See the beauty of life and all its glory, and you will be able to feel that innate sense of serenity. This state of mind is not reserved for only a select few. Peace of mind is the goal of every human being. And, like the sun, it is always there, if only you can wait for the clouds, and your negative thoughts, to dissipate. By not taking the clouds, and your negative thoughts seriously, you will allow yourself the opportunity to feel calm, relaxed, serene, and at peace with the world.

I. LOVE & FORGIVENESS

When love fills the heart there is no need to judge yourself or others; happiness takes over and contaminated, negative thoughts vanish.

Choose love over hatred and blame.
You will then feel good about life, and you will be able to find goodness in others.
Life is too short to live it with anger, conflict, and ill will. Learn, instead, to live a life giving of yourself to others - without expecting anything in return. You will then feel satisfaction, fulfillment, and joy in your heart.

When you forgive yourself and others for past hurts and mistakes you will free yourself of unnecessary pain and anguish. When you hang on to unforgiveness over yesterday's mistakes and hurtful remarks, you are depriving yourself of a life of contentment in the here and now.
Yesterday's pain and difficulties are merely today's memories, only thoughts about past experiences. They have nothing to do with seeing the wonder of life today. When you find forgiveness in your heart, you release feelings of resentment and bitterness. In so doing, you allow your natural loving feelings to bring harmony in your life.

Portland, Oregon

J. GRATITUDE

Many people feel that their lives would be more fulfilling and enjoyable if only they had more money, a bigger house, more friends, or a better job. But it all boils down to how you look at life now, without fretting about what you don't have.

Gratitude is the best attitude. Instead of dwelling on the one or two areas of your life that are not satisfying, why not appreciate all that you do have in life.

Your life is already wonderful and fulfilling, if you only take the time to reflect on it. It is simply a matter of changing your habit of focusing on what is wrong or lacking in your life, and shifting your attention, instead, on all that you have achieved or accomplished. No, there is no law that says you have to constantly compare yourself with others.

Ironically, it often seems that when you shift your attention away from what you don't have and wish you had, to all that you do have, instead, you end up getting more of what you want anyway.

When feeling stressed, unhappy, or frustrated, simply try to entertain thoughts of gratitude for the people and the pleasant experiences in your life. You may find yourself on your way to a life of personal contentment, satisfaction, and enjoyment.

Montana de Oro, California

San Simeon, California

Chapter 8

Managing your Neurotransmitters

Now that I have you all relaxed and in a good mood, let us turn to a scientific topic: "neurotransmitters." Don't be alarmed, I'm not going to be esoteric or confusing in discussing this important subject. I just want to tell you about a function of our brain controlling how we act, think and feel. In other words, chemical reactions taking place in our brains that affect us in both, negative and positive ways.

I have emphasized the importance of thought behind our moods and feelings, however, there are some brain-related functions affecting us and the way we manage stress. According to an online article from Integrative Psychiatry.net, neurotransmitters are defined as:

"...powerful chemicals that regulate numerous physical and emotional processes such as mental performance, emotional states and pain response. Virtually all functions in life are controlled by neurotransmitters. They are the brain's chemical messengers. Interactions between neurotransmitters, hormones, and the brain chemicals have a profound influence on overall health and well-being. When our concentration and focus is good, we feel more directed, motivated, and vibrant. Unfortunately, if neurotransmitter levels are inadequate these energizing and motivating signals are absent and we feel more stressed and out-of-control."

Without going into a long dissertation on the many different kinds of neurotransmitters, I want to walk you through five of the major ones. They are:

Glutamate
Norepinephrine (also known as noradrenaline)
GABA (Gamma amino butyric acid)
Serotonin
Dopamine

These particular neurotransmitters are very important because they play a major role in our moods, and our mental health. They relate to good and poor mental health and to addictions.

Without getting too scientific or unnecessarily complicated, I would like to define each of these chemical reactors in simple, down-to-earth language. The following descriptions can be found on Integrative Psychiatry.net.

Glutamate is a major excitatory neurotransmitter of the brain. It is necessary for us to learn and to remember things. When you feel tired and demonstrate poor brain activity, it's usually because you are experiencing low levels of glutamate. On the other hand, very high levels can kill neurons (nerve cells) in the brain. Imbalances in glutamate levels relate to many neurodegenerative diseases, including Alzheimer's disease and Parkinson's. Depression, obsessive-compulsive disorder and Autism are also related to high levels of glutamate.

Another excitatory neurotransmitter is norepinephrine also know in Great Britain as noradrenaline. High levels of norepinephrine are associated with stress, anxiety, hyperactivity and high blood pressure. Low levels are associated with lack of motivation, lack of energy and lack of focus.

While glutamate and norepinephrine tend to excite us and I don't necessarily mean sexually, other neurotransmitters are part of what is commonly referred to as the inhibitory system.

One major inhibitory neurotransmitter is GABA or Gamma amino butyric acid. Its major role is in helping the body's neurons recover after transmission by slowing us down. It helps reduce anxiety and stress. It functions as a significant mood modulator and helps regulate norepinephrine, adrenaline, dopamine and serotonin.

Another very important inhibitory neurotransmitter is serotonin. Mood problems often surface in people due to a serotonin imbalance. When in balance, serotonin can help defend against anxiety and depression. If there is a shortage of serotonin in the body, individuals can experience a sad depressed mood, high anxiety and even panic attacks. Shortages can also contribute to migraine headaches, sleeping problems, obsession or compulsions, feeling tense and irritable, the craving of sweets and reduce interest in sex. In addition, one's hormones and estrogen levels can affect serotonin levels and may explain why some women have premenstrual and menopausal mood problems. Furthermore, daily stress can significantly reduce one's serotonin levels.

Finally, there is the very important neurotransmitter dopamine. It has a chemical structure similar to epinephrine and norepinephrine. Its major function, generally speaking, is to activate other neurotransmitters and aid in exploratory behavior and pleasure-seeking behaviors. It tends to balance serotonin. While low levels have been connected to Parkinson's disease, high levels of dopamine have been linked to Autism, mood swings, attention deficit disorder in children and to Schizophrenia and other forms of psychosis.

A person's motivation, interest and drive are associated with dopamine. From a positive stress standpoint, adequate dopamine levels contribute to love, exercising, listening to music and sex. Insufficient amounts of dopamine may be responsible for poor concentration, low energy levels, a lack of motivation and difficulty in completing tasks.

In essence, the neurotransmitter serotonin is associated with the general feeling of well being while dopamine is associated with pleasure and elation. Why do I bring this up? Because serotonin and dopamine are two of about six neurotransmitters associated with addiction, particularly alcohol and drugs. It is commonly known our bodies have a reward pathway to the brain. Aside from alcohol and drugs being a part of this pathway, so is food, particularly sugar. The argument by some is that sugar can be addicting. If the pleasure center of our brains is not getting enough of some substances, then our body experiences a deficit. What I want to emphasize about stress is the problem with addiction in general. One contributing reason many scientists and health professionals view alcoholism as a disease, is the notion of craving. Why do some people seem to crave alcohol and drugs, and certain foods like chocolate? The reason, in part, seems related to both serotonin and dopamine levels. If the body has low levels of one or both of these neurotransmitters, then the need for raising the levels seems paramount to our stress reduction and happiness. This is especially the case for dopamine. Some people believe alcoholism, and other addictions, relate to a concept referred to as dopamine deficiency.

Thus, an individual may start out wanting or more accurately, needing to raise his or her dopamine level to satisfy the neural reward pathway to the brain. Individuals may do this by drinking alcohol or by ingesting drugs like marijuana or cocaine. Unfortunately, a vicious cycle is created. While people may start out getting high by taking these substances, they end up taking them in order not to feel low. When they do this, the cycle becomes endless. The more your body and you want something to feel pleasure and satisfaction, the less you feel fulfilled. As a result, dependence and addiction may set in. It has been suggested by some scientists that alcoholics and other addicts may have inherited a gene or genes related to the dopamine deficiency problem. The argument then is made that addicts can't help it and no matter what they do, they will always be labeled alcoholics or addicts. This may be the prevailing rationale for the need of Alcoholics Anonymous (AA) and other support groups.

Over the years, I have had great appreciation for AA or any other support group. Furthermore, after providing extensive outpatient and inpatient psychotherapy to alcoholics, I reached the same conclusion as most of my counterparts that alcoholism is a disease. It has an etiology, a cause that has classic symptoms, and is treatable. Similarly, I have provided therapy to countless people with a variety of addictions.

When I mention treatment for alcoholics and addicts, I am referring to the kinds of treatment also provided to other mental health related problems. Treatment could be in the form of counseling and psychotherapy, as well as medications. While there are many benefits to effective counseling and psychotherapy, there is something to be said for a popular class of prescription medications known technically as Selective Serotonin-Reuptake Inhibitors (SSRIs). They include Prozac, Zoloft, Lexapro and Paxil. These medications are primarily used to help combat depression. However, some drugs like Paxil are used to help treat depression and anxiety.

Additionally, you have a variety of medications called anxiolytics like Xanax and Valium, which primarily are used to treat anxiety. These particular medications are technically referred to as Benzodiazepines. They can become habit forming and pharmaceutical companies have developed less habit-forming drugs for anxiety, for example, Buspar.

There are a large number of other medications used for the treatment of depression. They may have a greater effect on other neurotransmitters. For example, there is Wellbutrin, which is a Selective Dopamine-Reuptake Inhibitor (SDRI).Then there is the popular anti-depressant drug called Cymbalta, which is a Selective Serotonin Norepinephrine Reuptake Inhibitor (SNRI).

I don't bring up the names of these drugs and their respective classifications just for your own edification, nor do I discuss them to try and confuse you. The reason I bring them up is simple—popularity. These medications can be and have proven to be effective in treating mental illness, namely depression and anxiety. As I mentioned, there is also the availability of counseling and psychotherapy. There was a time when psychiatrists provided psychoanalysis and other forms of psychotherapy. Since the 1960s, however, things in the mental health field have changed dramatically. Many other professionals have entered the field, including clinical psychologists, psychotherapists, marriage and family counselors and social workers. Today, these other mental health field experts provide much of the outpatient treatment of mental health related problems. For a variety of reasons, many psychiatrists today provide more drug therapy than outpatient therapy.

One reason for the shift in focus is the wide availability of medications prescribed by medical doctors other than psychiatrists. Among others, they may include internists and family physicians. It seems the stigma of receiving psychotherapy or medication from a psychiatrist still exists. This factor, coupled with the need for an instant fix or cure, has led to a burgeoning of psychotropic drug prescriptions. While many people with mental health and addiction type problems continue to make weekly visits to a mental health professional, there seems to be an increasing number of people who seek treatment from their family physician in the way of prescription medications. Obviously, people do not have appropriate health coverage for outpatient psychotherapy or simply can't afford it. Unfortunately, a large number of people go without any kind of treatment for their mental health related problems.

I do not see why an individual can't have a choice or option when it comes to getting help for their problems. I see nothing wrong with a person choosing to see their family physician or a psychiatrist for that matter, instead of seeking help from a psychologist or social worker. The point I am trying to make is there are a variety of ways to resolve problems with moods or with anxiety. Since many of these problems stem from high levels of stress, I feel the need to reiterate what I've been saying all along, LOOK FOR WAYS TO REDUCE STRESS!

A person may be vulnerable to mental health related problems, including alcoholism and other addictions for a variety of reasons. They include heredity, upbringing, traumatic life experiences, etc. It gets back to the age-old discussion of "nature vs. nurture." One person susceptible to problems stemming from daily stress could be because of his nature—heredity. His or her genetic makeup may determine the way the neurotransmitters work. In effect, one could be born with a lower than normal level of serotonin and dopamine. Yet, another person may stress out because of childhood abuse, poor upbringing or other environmentally related problems.

It seems it doesn't make much difference as to why one person is more easily upset with stress compared to the next person. What is important is the way each person reacts to the stressors in his or her life. As we have been discussing, there are many good ways to combat stress, including thought recognition, exercise and relaxation. You might say, "Yes, you already told me about that, but what does that have to do with neurotransmitters?"

Well, the tools and techniques I have been recommending to help reduce stress all have an effect on your neurotransmitters. This is especially true for the serotonin, dopamine and GABA levels in your body. If the levels are too low, we can help increase them through psychotropic medications or by ingesting alcohol and other substances. One could also benefit from participating in "talk therapy." In other words, there are choices and alternatives to use to help reduce anxiety or raise mood levels. Just because you may have been unlucky to inherit a gene for alcoholism, if there truly is such a thing, not all is doomed.

Similarly, even though one of your parents or grandparents

was anxious, hyper or depressed most of the time, does not mean you are a helpless victim. Furthermore, you don't necessarily have to depend on medication to control your symptoms. While anti-depressants or anti-anxiety drugs serve their purpose and may at times help modulate your neurotransmitters, it does not mean you have to be permanently dependent upon them. Don't get me wrong, whether or not you take medications to help calm you down or lift your spirits does not mean your neurotransmitters will be completely balanced. In other words, no matter what means of action you take to reduce or control stress, you may never be completely free of its affects. Maybe the best you can hope for is to feel less depressed or less anxiety-stricken. That's okay because in reality there is no panacea or magic bullet when it comes to finding physiological or psychological balance in life.

Whether you use natural or artificial means to facilitate brain chemistry balance, the ideal goal seems to be to enhance one's emotional well-being. I'd like to quote from the book, "Spontaneous Happiness" (2011) by the famous integrative physician, Andrew Weil, M.D. It's a message I have been trying to emphasize throughout this book:

"Chemical imbalances in the brain may well correlate with depression, anxiety, and other emotional disturbances, but the arrows of cause and effect can point in both directions. Optimizing emotional wellness, as by improving attention, changing destructive patterns of thinking, and finding contentment within, can also optimize brain chemistry, correcting any deficiencies in neurotransmitters."

Take work related pressure, for example. Even with all the tools, medications, exercise and meditation techniques at our disposal, we can't accurately predict how you or others will react to a given stress-related situation. You may know yourself pretty well and may have a good idea how you tend to react to stress at work or at home. As far as judging others, we can only speculate how they deal with stress. In other words, by observing others' behavior, we can only assume how they will react under pressure.

As an example, let's take the popular ESPN TV and radio Sports Talk Show, "Mike and Mike in the Morning." The show's two hosts, Mike Greenberg and Mike Golic are very popular with listeners and viewers alike. They are well respected by other sports announcers and athletes. Their radio-TV show comes on very early each week day morning from 6 to 10 am, eastern time. Presumable, they have to wake up early and drive to work in time for the show, which are stressors in and of themselves. Additionally, they have to stay on top of current sports related events, topics and controversies.

Take the NFL draft, for instance. The first round of the annual draft took place on prime time, on a Friday. Mike Greenberg commented on having to attend to some family matters during the NFL draft broadcast on a Friday night. He said he used his BlackBerry to find out about who was drafted during the first round. Presumable, he was under some stress. For example, pressure to try and stay current while having to be responsible for some family matters. I know over the years, both Mike Greenberg and Mike Golic utilize one of their program-sponsored pieces of workout equipment. They apparently exercise when they can and that can be a good way to reduce their job related stress.

In observing the two "Mikes" on TV, without trying to analyze them, there is no noticeable strain in their facial or verbal expressions. They do exhibit some testy, occasionally defensive behavior at times. That seems to be part of the program, bantering of verbal exchanges between them. They have some obvious personality differences between them. For example, Greenberg comes across as being more sensitive at times while Golic appears to be more aggressive. They are intelligent, knowledgeable, articulate and able to overcome their disagreements. In short, they demonstrate good chemistry together, which makes for good ESPN ratings for the show.

However, there is the pressure of providing analysis of various sports teams and events with a huge number of details and facts. They have to present the program material in a fast-paced fashion in order to keep the audience's interest. Even though we can only speculate, it would appear both Mikes handle the stress associated with their show very well.

The experience of doing such a show can raise one's norepinephrine level and get one's adrenaline flowing. It can also raise the serotonin and dopamine levels. They must enjoy hosting such a show and must have their neurotransmitters in balance or they could become vulnerable to burnout.

What does a TV show like, "Mike and Mike in the Morning" have to do with neurotransmitters? Well, for one thing, viewers like myself feel the show raises their serotonin and dopamine levels, in a natural kind of way. Watching this TV program or any other program or movie that helps one come away with a feel good response is good for one's mental health. Such programs help reduce stress in your life while keeping your neurotransmitters in balance. Remember serotonin is associated with the general feeling of well being while dopamine helps contribute to feelings of pleasure and elation. If watching a TV program or movie with your spouse or other loved ones can increase these two neurotransmitters in such a natural way, without artificial substances, so much the better for you and for others in society.

On the other hand, if watching a violent, disturbing program or movie causes you to feel upset, anxious or even depressed, avoid watching such shows. They will only disrupt the flow of your neurotransmitters and thereby contribute to uneasy and distressed thoughts and feelings. All of us have seen movies with sad or depressing endings. You can even go online to find lists of such movies. Two examples are, "They Shoot Horses,

Don't They" (1969), which is about dancing marathons for enjoyment and money during the Great Depression, and the recent "Shutter Island" (2010). This movie is about the investigation of a murderess who escaped from a hospital for the criminally insane. I think these two examples may qualify for the negative movie list.

On the other hand, a couple of movies making the list of feel good movies would be, "While You Were Sleeping" (1995), and more recently, the popular movie, "The King's Speech" I(2010). If at all possible, and if it's in the realm of your control or choosing, stick with feel good TV programs and movies.

To emphasize my point, Dr. Andrew Weil puts it very succinctly when he says in his book, "Spontaneous Happiness"_ if you:

"...habitually and unconsciously listen to sad music, read sad stories, and watch sad movies, chances are you will be sadder than if you choose happier input. If you habitually tune in to news programs that make you angry and distraught, chances are you will spend less time in the zone of serenity and contentment. The challenge is to exercise conscious control over what you pay attention to. The world is both wonderful and terrible, beautiful and ugly. At any moment one can choose to focus on the positive and the negative aspects of reality."

In summary, it is important to participate in those daily activities that will lower your GABA and norepinephrine levels when you feel anxiety stricken, and raise your serotonin and dopamine levels when you are feeling low. In addition to engaging in various activities to maintain good brain chemistry balance, it is equally important to open up and simply talk to someone about the things troubling you. As a result, you may feel good about yourself and your life.

Generally speaking, any activity you do actively or passively to help lower your stress level by regulating your neurotransmitters in effective, beneficial ways can lead to better physical and mental health. Such activity could include exercise, like the naturally occurring runner's high when jogging, walking or participating in sporting events. I'm all for raising your dopamine level without the use of dope in any natural way that suits your fancy.

Chapter 9

Slow Down and Enjoy Life

We have covered a great deal of information about stress and its relation to our thinking, emotions and lives in general. One major aspect related to stress is mood. When we say a person is in a good or bad mood, what are we talking about? There are all kinds of definitions of mood. You can find them in various psychology textbooks, websites and in other books unrelated to psychology. I like to think of mood as a feeling state that predominates our life at a certain time. It could last for a few minutes, days, even years.

The funny thing about moods is they not only affect the person experiencing a mood state, but also those around him or her. That can include adults, children, parents, friends, etc. There is the old saying, "If mamma ain't happy, ain't nobody happy." Of course, that could be fathers or husbands, not just mothers and wives. It seems inevitable if a loved one is in a low mood, we become drawn into that mood as well. What we need to realize is another person's mood has absolutely nothing to do with us. As I have already emphasized, it's not what other people say or do that affects us, it's our thought about their remarks or behavior. The same can be said for another person's moods.

At this point, you may vehemently disagree with me. You may say something like, "Sure, you don't have to live with this person." That is very true! There is however another way to look at it.

I am not the only one who believes we allow ourselves to become part of another person's mood state. If I may, I'd like to quote again, from what Richard Carlson and Joseph Bailey have to say in their excellent book, "Slowing Down to the Speed of Life" (1997). They're of the opinion that you don't need to:

"...take other people's low moods personally. Instead of being defensive, judgmental, or frightened of their moods, try to have some compassion. Being patient with another's mood isn't something you can, 'think' your way into. You have to see that your mate is just off; no big deal – it happens to the best of us. Wait a few minutes or hours, and you'll be in a low mood too!"

Carlson and Bailey go on to say you should, "...try to see another's negativity as impersonal, even when it is directed at you personally." They refer to this notion as being immune to low moods. They point out, "other people's low moods have nothing to do with us; they are a product of their thinking." If you think about it, you are feeling stressed out over the other person's moods. You are thinking about how bad it is and how miserable or disturbing your life is all because he or she may have a mood swing or simply be in occasionally bad moods.

You might ask, "How come my mate is in a low mood anyway?" For that matter, you might wonder why anyone has low moods. Is it because of work related problems? Is it because of the kids? Is it your fault for not getting dinner ready on time or because you failed to pay a certain bill on time? The list could be endless. When you come down to it, we tend to blame the reason for the mood on something, someone or some event that's out there, external to us. One explanation for any mood to surface, good or bad, is because we are human. We're just wired that way. So what? We as human beings are subject to mood swings in general, often for no observable or obvious cause.

Often, moods just come and go at random for no identifiable reason. WHAT MATTERS IS NOT THE MOOD, BUT OUR REACTION TO IT. How do we deal with our many different, sometimes low moods? How do we act or behave when someone else is in an angry, bad mood? Learn to separate yourself from others, what's theirs is not yours.

From my point of view, the one major thing you can do is to notice or observe your thought about the mood level of the other person or of yourself. It gets back to what I have already talked about regarding such things as thought processes and getting back to the moment. Another very important thing you can do is to learn how to slow yourself down and enjoy life. When you do, you'll be pleasantly surprised by how well you can avoid being so troubled by your negative moods or by the low moods of others. That is the crux of this chapter. I already discussed the problem of living life in the fast lane. Now, I want to elaborate on how we can reduce the tendency to ride the fast lane, to, instead, travel life more in the slow lane.

I want to emphasize there is nothing wrong with spending some time in the fast paced lane of life. I say some time because once again, I want to point out the need for balance in our lives. It sure is fun to keep busy at times, take the kids to a football game, attend a basketball game with friends, etc. Similarly, you can spend many hours at work doing the things you enjoy doing there and enjoy being part of a work team or project that consumes you. Besides, you may even get an occasional ego boost by completing job related tasks in a thorough, highly competent and timely fashion.

When you're enjoying life so much with busy, active and time-consuming events, and with other, fun-loving people, why should you take time to slow down? At this point, you may ask, "How can one slow down and enjoy life?" That is a good question. You'll notice I didn't entitle this chapter, "Slow Down to Enjoy Life." No, I purposely meant to label it, "Slow Down and

Enjoy Life" because I really believe you can do both. I think it's very important to slow down for the following reasons:

- Improve mood level
- Improve physical health
- Calm one's nerves
- Decrease restlessness
- Enjoy and enhance relationships
- Allow new, innovative, and creative ideas to surface
- Enjoy the natural beauty around us (smell the roses)
- Maintain focus on the present moment

These are just some reasons for slowing down your life. After giving it some thought, you may be able to add to the list some of your own reasons for wanting or needing to slow down. No matter how conscientious or responsible you feel, you need to be as a spouse, parent, friend and worker; you need to take time out for yourself. In other words, from time-to-time, you may need to take a break from the hustle and bustle of being a caregiver, partner, friend and loyal employee.

Any problems you may need to attend to at work or home will still be there, after you get back to being there for others. Don't get me wrong, I am not advocating being selfish, lazy or for having a devil may care attitude. It all gets back to bringing more balance in your life. When you take some time to relax and enjoy your hobby or other interest, and then return to being a good partner, parent and employee, you will be in a more positive mood and thereby be more loving, caring and productive at work.

I'm not just suggesting taking like a fifteen-minute or an hour break. In the same vein, I'm not suggesting you can find enjoyment in life only when you take breaks or time out for yourself. No, you can find consistent enjoyment in your life no matter where you are or whom you are with. Suppose, for example, you are at work. You have one main boss, along with others who may think they're your boss by looking to you for help in completing a task. Let's suppose one of the other "bosses" requests your assistance on a project and the task must be carried out by next Monday.

You have some choices to make. I say choices because the day before, another "boss" came to you with a different request. Additionally, last week, a third "boss" came to you with another request. You have at least three staff members wanting your help or assistance. They each want the work done right and they want it now. What do you do? Well, let's try to put into practice some of the ideas I have been suggesting you do to help reduce stress.

Remember, our objectives include catching your negative thoughts about what others say or do, getting back to the moment, avoiding "Agitated Avenue," enjoying life and finding balance in life. With this job scenario in mind, you could step back in your mind, take a deep breath, then respond to each of the three co-workers with agreeableness, but with some degree of assertiveness. You could tell the first person you'll have the project task completed by May 10th. You then tell the next person their part of the project will be completed by May 20th and tell the third person the job will be completed by May 30th.

Any one or more of these three workers may get frustrated or angry with you for not prioritizing their particular job task or even threaten to complain to your immediate supervisor about the situation. Other people in your shoes may become defensive, angry and stressed out to the point of going to pieces. Not you, because you are able to notice some negative, unpleasant thoughts about the work situation surfacing and immediately calm yourself down and react rationally. To be able to do this effectively, you will need to find that balance we have been talking about. By learning to slow down, take life easier when you can, to take your negative thoughts more casually and less seriously, you can lower your stress level, and be more effective in dealing with situations like the one at work I just described.

The upshot of all this discussion on slowing down is to try and get you off the treadmill of life and reduce your stress level in the process. This is much better than raising your stress level through excessive work or by filling your plate with extra activities and burdens.

Let's talk some more about enjoyment. We already discussed some ways to find enjoyment through a brisk walking program or other exercise activities. However, there are things you can do to bring sheer joy to your life. Some people believe you can only find true joy from within your own heart and soul. What does that mean exactly? To me, it means finding satisfaction, even pleasure, by looking inside yourself. You don't necessarily need outside entertainment, material things, social or sports activities to find joy in your life. Many people think they need material things and entertainment to find happiness. People think they need new cars, houses, a new computer, a new iPod, big screen TV, etc. While these things bring temporary pleasure to us, they only last so long. After purchasing a new TV, car, motorcycle, etc., after awhile, perhaps a few weeks or more, what happens? The pleasure wears off. Then we're off buying the next new thing. For example, maybe the iPhone 4 is no longer satisfying, so you're off buying the iPhone 5.The cycle becomes endless. It seems the more we have, the more we need to get or acquire for us to be satisfied.

One of the reasons why people cling to a busy lifestyle, one that is surrounded by friends, things, events, etc. is because of BOREDOM. Some mental health specialists believe boredom is a result of inner frustration and despair. They think the need for outside things and social activity is merely a temporary distraction from some inner pain and emptiness. They say true happiness comes from being, not doing. I agree with this conclusion about boredom to some extent, but we can only speculate what the true reason or cause is for boredom. Furthermore, it's hard to make sweeping generalizations.

It seems to me the real reason for anyone's boredom can vary from person to person. It really doesn't matter why you may be bored. But, if you can only find temporary enjoyment in doing things by joining clubs, playing video games, etc., then it's time to look at finding longer lasting, perhaps, permanent happiness by trying some of the following suggestions, paraphrased in part from a Website entitled, "How to Get More Enjoyment Out of Every Day" by Jonathan.

A. **Find Simplicity** – Learn to quiet your mind and restore a sense of order to your life. Set a goal to "declutter" your mind and your environment. That means trying to at least reduce the accumulation of physical, mental, and emotional clutter in your life. In this busy, hectic, over stimulated world, simple activities and events can be truly experienced and enjoyable if you focus on the, "quality" of the activity, and not just on the, "quantity" of material things and events.

B. **Experience the Activity** – Instead of doing one thing and thinking about another, remind yourself of the need to get, "back to the moment." How can you enjoy one activity when your mind is somewhere else. This is a distraction! Even the most mundane, even routine activity can be enjoyable if you allow yourself to stay focused on it. When you really experience an activity, by taking it all in so to speak, you are really living life.

C. **Savor the Flavor** – Take time to slow down and take in the little things, one at a time. What this means is to savor the tiny pieces of fruit, or to enjoy a cup of coffee or tea, one bite or sip at a time. Try not to "gulp" your food down. Nutritionists tell us that taking tiny bites at a time will slow you down, eat less, and gain less weight in the process. Similarly, try not to rush through a particular activity, just to get it done. Don't be in such a hurry. Enjoy each particle of food or individual activity by letting your senses, see, hear, touch, and feel each one – in the moment.

D. **Add Variety to Life** – In addition to your routine activities, add some variety. Life is too short, so try something new. Take a different vacation from the normal one of going to the same beach, city, state, or hotel. Instead of going to work via the same route, try a different street or highway. Instead of turning on the television and watching the same program or news broadcast, take a walk or go outside to play on the swing set with the kids. Now is the time to try that "something" you always wanted to do, but could never find the time to get around to it.

E. **Do What You Love** – While it's important to take care of your, "to do" list, and to attend to other responsibilities, you need to take some time out to do the things that excite you. If you can't do the things you like to do, then you may begin to resent your life. So, it's important to find that balance again, between doing what you have to, and doing what you want to.

F. **Reduce Commitments** – Try to reduce or minimize the things that merely consume your time and energy. While it may be necessary to commit to some things, many so-called "obligations" are not really required. For each commitment or obligation that comes your way, ask yourself if it will fulfill and enhance your life, or will it just add stress to your life? If you don't see any positive benefits to it, and if other people in your life will not be negatively affected, then refuse to do it.

G. **Focus on the What's Important** – Ask yourself if some of the things you do on a daily basis are all that important. Do you really need to spend hours and hours texting, using Twitter or Facebook? Obviously, if your livelihood depends on a certain activity, let's say talking on the phone for telemarketing purposes, then that's important for productivity. But, for others, spending hours on the cell phone, or the computer may be a distraction from doing the things that really matter in your life.

H. **Let Go and Relax** – Your body needs to relax along with your mind. But it can't if your mind is busy obsessing over all the things you didn't do or finish today. Your body and the corresponding muscles will only relax if you just allow your mind to let go of unpleasant thoughts, worries, or anything else that may cause you stress. If you take some time each day to practice letting go, you will find greater enjoyment in life.

Finding enjoyment in life varies for each one of us. There is one activity I have found enjoyable and virtually stress-free over most of my lifetime, which is photography. I find this hobby to be relaxing at times, exciting at other times, and very fulfilling. I have enjoyed taking photos of people, animals, fish, buildings, and of course, various landscapes. This kind of activity helps free me from more busy activity and is very rewarding in general.

It need not be an either or situation for you. That is, an activity is not necessarily all stressful or filled with joy. No matter the situation or activity, there will be good moments and days, followed by bad moments and days. This is where finding balance comes into play again. Let me share with you my own personal experience. My wife and I were avid campers for years. We bought and sold at least three travel trailers over the years, ending up with a 26' trailer.

While my wife thoroughly enjoyed camping, as did our three sons on numerous occasions, I found it stressful at times, but relaxing and enjoyable at other times. It was particularly stressful for me to pull a big trailer down the highway, often times in busy traffic. Then there was the hooking up of the trailer, unhooking it, setting it up, going for water, etc. Nevertheless, once these duties were completed, with the help of my wife and kids, I found it relatively easy to relax and enjoy the campfire, the hikes in the beautiful forests, walking along the beach, taking walks in the campground and enjoying the moonlit sky at night. You see, it is possible to find balance between the stressful, anxiety-ridden activity and its other, more positive and rewarding parts.

There is one other very important activity that needs some discussion, SEX. If you are to find great satisfaction and outright pleasure in sex, it is incumbent upon you to slow down and get back to the moment. I'm referring to those intimate moments. When you and your partner are relaxed, not busy fussing over household chores, tending to the cooking or putting the kids to bed, you are more apt to find some good, sexual time for each other.

When you and your loved one are alone in bed, free of outside distractions, then you can unwind, relax and enjoy each other's bodies. Oh yes, this is the time for gentle embrace, sensuous touches, romantic kissing and passionate sexual intercourse!

Couples can and do practice effective sexual techniques to lengthen the time and quality of the sexual response. Some techniques are designed to slow the man down so the woman can truly enjoy the anticipated climax. This may include what the experts refer to as the "squeeze technique" of the head of the penis and finger manipulation of the clitoris.

Whatever the couple finds satisfactory and painless can be discovered together if you just take the time to enjoy each other and the sex act itself. Having an orgasm may be the ultimate goal, but getting there is half the fun. Take the time to bring rapture and pleasure to each other and truly enjoy each other's relationship in every way possible.

When you are able to bring balance between work and recreation into your life, you will find it easier to deal with stress. When you are able to slow down and enjoy life, you will experience a sense of peace and harmony.

Chapter 10
Gratitude is the Attitude

Some people are of the opinion or belief that life sucks. They not only have a difficult time finding enjoyment in life, but also lack gratitude for life. In short, they have a negative attitude toward life. While a more positive person might see the glass half-full, a negatively oriented person might see it as being half-empty. However, many people tend to fall somewhere in the middle. They have many days where they find fault with their lives, with others or with the circumstances of their lives. Other days, more positive thoughts about themselves, others or about life in general fill their minds.

We have already discussed moods and their effect on people. There is also something to be said for attitude. What is attitude anyway? It's a state of mind. While moods are feeling states that may come and go for no apparent reason, one's attitude tends to remain stable or consistent over time. We generally view people as having either a negative attitude or a positive attitude. This is generally applied to their point of view or outlook toward life.

If a person has a bad or negative attitude, he or she tends to see only the bad in others. As such, they tend to be critical of others, even of themselves and easily find faults and weaknesses in others. They have no appreciation for others and their opinions and really don't have much appreciation for life in general. Furthermore, they may even be difficult to live or work with, and may tend to alienate others.

Most of us have known people who can be categorized as having a negative attitude. You may wonder how and why people have this kind of attitude. Is it something they're born with or is it the result of upbringing? Well, actually, it may be a combination of the two. For instance, a person may be viewed as being closed minded or disagreeable. These two characteristics are traits and sometimes considered by psychologists as being part of a cluster of traits that make up one's personality. By virtue of basic personality type, a person may tend to exhibit more openness to ideas, new experiences, be accepting of others, etc., compared to another person. Similarly, a person may tend to be more agreeable, that is, easier to get along with and be with compared to another person.

While genetics may play a role in determining which one a person may turn out to be in life, other factors can enter into play as well. Certainly, familial and parental influences can play a role in how open or agreeable a person may be, along with other possible reasons. In other words, people can and do change for the better.

One way for anyone to change is to find GRATITUDE in life. A person with a negative attitude, one with the two negative personality traits I mentioned, may learn to become a little more open to other's ideas, opinions and beliefs. This person may also learn to get along better with others, to be more agreeable when communicating with others. This may necessitate an open mind, and a willingness to change. Nevertheless, this takes practice and in time, it will become a habit.

Instead of harboring negative feelings about others or about life in general, a person who develops a sense of gratitude in life will notice it's his or her own thoughts getting in the way. Instead, they become focused on the positive thoughts about others and about life in general. When they are able to do this, their attitude changes. They will then be more conscious of the good things in life.

Gratitude is not something related to having possessions or successes in life. It's not all about what you have in life or don't have in life that determines one's level of appreciation. It's good to appreciate the finer things in life, but one need not depend on them in order to feel gratitude. If you do have many treasures in life and have people doing nice things for you, that's fine. Yes, you should extend a thank you for these things and to people who do good things for you.

You can find the feeling of gratitude inside of yourself. It's always been there because it's part of nature. It's part of being a human being. You were born with the capacity for gratitude. You may not have noticed the feeling because your thoughts about problems, negative events and experiences have gotten in the way. You may have allowed the negative aspects of your life to consume you.

It may be beneficial for you to set aside some gratitude sessions. From time to time, take inventory of the wealth of good things in your life. Personally, I try to make time to say, "Thank you, God" for everything in my life. My personal list includes my wife, three sons, four grandchildren, and my health. Just look at all you have to be thankful for, then let the feelings of gratitude take over. You don't need things and certain circumstances or conditions for you to feel appreciation for life. Look how many people in the world who may have fewer possessions or who may be living in less than ideal circumstances or situations, but who still feel and express a deep sense of gratitude for life. Such people aren't fooling themselves. They possess a positive attitude toward life. They look at what they have, which may not seem like a lot, but they enjoy it, while others complain and mutter about that which they don't have.

Learn to pay attention to the positive thoughts and feelings in you so you can feel that sense of deep gratitude for life. At this point, if you were to walk around with this kind of positive attitude toward life, you would actually end up being selfless because you would be easier to hang out with and would be viewed as being more loving and caring. What do you have to offer others anyway? Well, it is your presence, your well-being, yourself and your good will.

In essence, if you feel good, then others around you feel good. Your good feeling rubs off on others. With gratitude comes joy and a good feeling of appreciation for life. Simply practice being kind to yourself and kind to others.

You may have noticed people who walk around with their heads down, not making eye contact with others. On the other hand, you may have seen people walking around with their heads held high, making eye contact with others and expressing kind and friendly words to others. What are we to conclude? We're not talking about a person who thinks well of him or herself, who is self -centered or arrogant. No, we're talking about a person who appears to have a zest for life, a positive attitude toward life and is nice and kind to others.

I'm not saying there is anything wrong with being shy and introverted, or that extraverted, outgoing people don't have low moods. Even if you're normally very outgoing, friendly and likeable, you can still find yourself walking around not wanting to reach out or make eye contact with others. Your mind may simply be on something else, maybe wondering if you paid the electric bill the other day. Whatever the reason, it's hard to judge people and their moods, much less their general attitude toward life. But when your normal, gregarious self is present, others do feel good when you acknowledge their existence.

To help us feel a sense of gratitude, God has endowed us with five senses. Why not use your sense of sight, hearing, smell, taste and touch to take in all that life has to offer. I use my senses to take in my environment. I also personally use my senses to absorb the great feeling of just being around my wife, Maureen. What comes to my mind is the late and great John Denver song, "Annie's Song." When I'm with my wife, I can almost use her name, "Maureen's Song" with the line, "You fill up my senses..."

You can thank God not only for the five senses, but also for a sixth sense, that being, "common sense." This is a simple, down-to-earth sense based on practical knowledge and judgment. Try to use it wisely as a means to living in a safe and reasonable manner.

If you are a person who harbors a great deal of resentment and has many regrets about your life, do some real soul-searching. Ask yourself if such negative thinking helps to find satisfaction and fulfillment in your life. There is the saying, "let go, let God in." There is a purpose for this kind of attitude. It enables you not only to "let 'ole dogs lay," but also find the elusive inner peace and tranquility. In short, go with the flow and let things work themselves out. If you have a problem that's been troubling you for a long time and you can't seem to find a solution, then even with a good attitude, there may not be a solution or answer. So, just let go!

Be grateful for what you have, instead of resentful for what you don't have. Being grateful is also a means to finding pleasure and comfort in life. When you free up your mind of all the bad and unpleasant things and bitterness you may have been feeling for years, you give yourself a new lease on life. In the same vein, if you stop beating yourself up for past mistakes, failures and inherent weaknesses, you will empower yourself with success. In other words, success is not necessarily in the doing but in the being. Just be and accept yourself for what you are with all the strengths and weaknesses you possess.

When you truly accept yourself, you find the inner quality of HUMILITY. Being humble is what Jesus Christ talked about and is a virtue praised by prophets and philosophers over the centuries. Feeling humble and interacting with others with humility is not a sign of weakness. The word humility means acting modestly and respectfully. It is probably the opposite of arrogance. People who act in a brash, arrogant, self-centered manner and who make a habit of bragging about how good or successful they are have a problem of some kind. They usually overcompensate for some inner fear, weakness or personal flaw. They not only fail to appreciate all the skills and riches they have, but they also show a lack of respect for others. You can be really good or skilled at something without having to laud it over everyone. Just simply enjoy all the natural talents and possessions you have and thank God for being so richly endowed.

Just as there are no two finger prints alike, so it is you will never be exactly the same as your parents or siblings. Thank the good Lord for your uniqueness. Think about it, there will never be another you on this earth again. You will be the only "one of a kind" who has ever walked the path you have chosen to take with your life. Choose your path wisely; learn to reduce the stress that may come along and always appreciate the things and people you discover along the path of life.

(Endnotes)

1 J.B. (1966), Psychological Monograhs: General and Applied, 80(1), 1-28, (Copyright © 1966 by the American Psychological Association. Adapted with permission)

Spontaneous Happiness" (2011) by Andrew Weil, M.D p.59-60
Spontaneous Happiness" (2011) by Andrew Weil, M.D p. 154

Testimonials

"Outstanding. Spot on and exactly what the doctor ordered at a time when Americans are more stressed out than ever. This is a must read. It explains in non-technical terms how each of us can deal with the stress we face in our daily lives."

Richard Clark
Member State Bar of Michigan & Adjunct Professor of Political Science

"This is a book I want all my patients to read. Its focus is on empowering individuals to cope with their daily and life-long stresses. Its style is an easy read, yet packed with data and insights. I have known and worked with Duane as a consulting psychologist for years."

William N. Nicholson, Ph.D., Neuropsychologist
President, Michigan Psychological Association

"A joy to read, this little book blends familiar examples, a conversational tone, decades of clinical experience, and REAL common sense. Pick it up, dive in, and strike a new and healthy balance in life."

Dale M. Herder, Ph.D.
English Professor, College Vice-President Emeritus, and Author

"What a great book! Duane Pajak has written a book that is both informative and helpful....it describes the three kinds of stress, 'frustration, pressure and conflict.' In addition, he illuminates the two kinds of thinking that we use, 'processing and free-flowing,' the former used in a more intentional way and the latter we commit to a subconscious mind that works on a concern while we go about doing other things in life. His book is helpful in how he gives practical suggestions to not only lessen stress but to actually use it in creative ways that deepen our lives."

Jerry Blevins
Retired College Professor of Religion

"This is an engaging, inspirational book for people…."

Philip Woollcott, M.D.
Retired Professor of Psychiatry
University of Illinois Chicago

"'It's All in Your Head' is a thoughtful, comprehensive, and readable summary of tried and true steps one can take to manage personal stress. I thoroughly enjoyed the easy-to-read 'free flow' masterpiece.

I highly recommend it."

Mary Lou Tanton
Retired Teacher

"Duane Pajak provides an easy-to-understand guide on how to manage stress. Reading his book is like having a conversation with a good friend on a front porch swing – relaxing and supportive! Duane provides helpful suggestions, tools and techniques readers can use to put themselves in control of their thoughts and feelings, thus keeping stress levels in check. Duane's approach is a holistic one, incorporating both physical and mental techniques such as yoga, walking, hiking, music, poetry and visualization. He is skilled at moving readers to see the importance of finding balance in their existence. Gratitude is a key factor in finding balance and leading a rewarding, abundant life; Duane provides tips on how to increase your sense of gratitude. Duane will help readers tune into their "natural wisdom" by learning that there is no such thing as a right or wrong way to look at things, but rather a different way of looking at things. In an age when it's easy to feel like you're spread too thin, Duane Pajak's book provides practical tools for taking life's daily challenges in stride."

Cameron Brunet-Koch, Ph.D., President
North Central Michigan College

About the Author

Duane Pajak has B.A. and M.A. degrees in psychology from Michigan State University. He has over thirty years of professional experience as a psychotherapist, CEO of two outpatient psychiatric clinics, and as an adjunct professor of psychology. He has taught psychology at several colleges and universities. Over the past several years, he has been an adjunct psychology professor at North Central Michigan College. In addition, he has given numerous talks and workshops on managing stress on the job and at home. In addition to his book, It's All in Your Head, he has an article published in the *The Sherlock Holmes Journal* of London (Winter, 2008). It is entitled, "Judge Sherlock Holmes for Yourself," and is an analysis and speculation of Sherlock Holmes' personality from the perspective of a personality test. Mr. Pajak has been married to Maureen for over forty-six years. They have three sons and four grandchildren. He makes his home in Michigan where he enjoys his life-long hobby of landscape photography.

CPSIA information can be obtained at www.ICGtesting.com
Printed in the USA
BVOW04s0620061113

335456BV00006B/123/P